Foreword

Waterford boasts a rich architectural heritage spanning many centuries. This heritage is the most tangible physical reminder of the culture, ideals, and history of a people now gone. Its appreciation and survival is a reflection of the values of the current generation into whose care this important historical evidence has been entrusted.

When posed with the question of what constitutes the architectural heritage, the most common response ranges from country houses to public buildings such as churches, courthouses, and town halls. While such buildings should be mentioned and appreciated for their inherent architectural and historical value, more modest artefacts are often overlooked and are therefore, arguably, at greater risk of being irredeemably lost.

In the course of the National Inventory of Architectural Heritage (NIAH) survey of the architectural heritage of County Waterford, carried out in 2003, a large number of building types were identified and recorded. For instance a rich, and generally unrecognised, collection of artefacts of interest and importance are located along the coastline and rivers of the county. Fishing ports on the coastline incorporate features typical of such settlements, including piers, quay walls, and boathouses. Lighthouses and navigational structures are sited on headlands and areas of potential danger to the mariner. The quays at Waterford City, considered to be amongst the most graceful in Europe, were also recorded as part of the survey. Inland, the remains of structures forming part of private ferry crossings flank the major rivers of the county, as at Villierstown and Camphire over the River Blackwater.

Special areas of interest, some unique to the county, were also identified as part of the NIAH survey. Portlaw, established in the early nineteenth century by the Malcomson family as a 'Model' village, features a range of structures that might be expected in more middle-size urban areas. The arrangement of civic, industrial, and private buildings in a carefully planned system distinguishes Portlaw in a national context.

Smaller scale items of importance include Waterford's stock of vernacular heritage, most commonly identified by the thatched cottage, but also including structures such as farm outbuildings. Once innumerable throughout the country, the last hundred years have witnessed a dramatic depletion in the numbers of thatched cottages surviving. Very few, depicted in archival sources, survive in the urban areas of the county. As a result, those that do remain are among the most important artefacts of the county's architectural heritage. Approximately one hundred have been included in the survey.

The purpose of the NIAH survey and the Introduction is to identify and highlight a representative selection of the architectural heritage of County Waterford. It is hoped that through raising awareness a better appreciation will be encouraged, together with a drive to protect the county's significant built heritage.

The NIAH survey of the architectural heritage of County Waterford can be accessed on the internet at:
www.buildingsofireland.ie

NATIONAL INVENTORY
of ARCHITECTURAL HERITAGE

MAP OF THE COUNTY
OF WATERFORD
(1824)

A map of Waterford, signed and dated by John Murray in 1824, outlines the baronies and towns of the county, together with topographical features including the main rivers and mountain ranges.

Courtesy of the Irish Architectural Archive.

Introduction

PARADE QUAY
Waterford
(c.1890)

An archival view of Parade
Quay depicts Reginald's
Tower in the foreground,
a collection of townhouses
on the site now occupied
by the Tower Hotel, and a
view up The Mall, the
street lined by formal
Georgian houses. The
steam yacht was a feature
of Waterford during a
period of busy commercial
activity on the quays.

*Courtesy of the National
Library of Ireland.*

County Waterford lies on the south-east coast of Ireland. Over the centuries the county's strategic coastal location has encouraged both invasion and settlement. This has facilitated its growth, and fostered links with communities and countries overseas. County Waterford is embraced by two mighty rivers, the Suir and the Blackwater, which almost delineate its boundaries with adjoining counties. With the exception of Waterford Harbour, which lies at the head of a scenic estuary, the coastline largely consists of small sheltered bays and ranges of low cliffs. The Knockmealdown, Monavullagh, and Comeragh Mountains rise to the north and west of the county with other upland areas, the Drum Hills, between Dungarvan and Youghal, County Cork. The fertile valleys of the Suir and Blackwater not only allow for rich arable land but have also provided the focus for centuries of human habitation; patterns that continue to this day.

(fig. 1)
ARDMORE CATHEDRAL
Ardmore
(fifth century)

The extensive ecclesiastical complex at Ardmore was established by Saint Declan in the fifth century; the church remained in use until 1838.

Courtesy of the Photographic Unit, Department of the Environment, Heritage and Local Government.

(fig. 2)
ARDMORE CATHEDRAL
Ardmore

Amid the carved detailing on the western wall of the cathedral, lunette panels depict biblical episodes including the story of the Adoration of the Magi, and the Judgement of Solomon.

Courtesy of the Photographic Unit, Department of the Environment, Heritage and Local Government.

People have lived in County Waterford for at least 7,000 years. In the 1980s the University of Sheffield's Ballylough Research Project uncovered significant supporting evidence for early settlement. Megalithic burial monuments survive around the eastern part of the county, along the coast, and on the banks of the River Suir. Indications of later settlement patterns include souterrains, underground passages often associated with ringforts or ecclesiastical sites. Evidence of an early watermill, dating to the ninth century, has been found at Ballydowane West. Waterford is rich in early ecclesiastical sites and that at Ardmore, founded by Saint Declan in the fifth century, has an outstanding Romanesque Cathedral *(figs. 1 - 2)*. Often reproduced in postcards and calendars, the site has assumed an almost iconic status in characterising a typical Irish building of this period. Other important sites include Lismore, where the cathedral was dedicated to Saint Mochuda. Although most early ecclesiastical sites in Waterford City have either been destroyed or subsumed into later structures, substantial ruins of some early Franciscan and Dominican friaries may still be seen.

Pre 1700

The geographical position of County Waterford facilitated the arrival of missionaries before the time of Saint Patrick. Both Ardmore and Lismore became sizeable settlements as their religious significance encouraged population growth. Such communities were threatened by the Viking incursions and yet it was from such an incursion that Waterford City, the region's largest urban centre, originated. Already established as Vadrarfjord by the Vikings at the end of the tenth century, the settlement, centred on an area close by Reginald's Tower, had become a large walled town by the time of the Anglo-Norman invasion in 1170. Waterford's significance as an important harbour and river crossing was consolidated thereafter. Extensive archaeological excavations since the 1980s continue to reveal more of the city's original fabric. Waterford and Dungarvan were the region's principal administrative centres in the Norman period; roles that continue to this day. Dungarvan grew up in the shadow of an important castle (after 1215) to become a port and walled market town. The unusual polygonal shell-keep of the castle is now a substantial ruin although remains of some later houses, possibly dating from the fifteenth or sixteenth century, may be seen on Castle Street and Quay Street. A prominently sited gabled market house, built on the site of its predecessor, shows the date 1690 on a roundel over the doorway; the building is now in use as an Arts Centre (2000) *(fig. 3)*. Tallow, another early settlement, was largely rebuilt during the seventeenth century when it was incorporated in 1615, by a charter of King James I (1566-1625), as the borough of 'Tallagh'. It served as an early centre of industry, being the site of ironworks controlled by Richard Boyle, 1st Earl of Cork (1566-1643).

In general County Waterford has known relatively few large-scale urban developments. By far the largest settlement, Waterford City, is complemented by a series of small towns and villages together with clusters of houses and farm buildings dotted across the landscape. Over the centuries the city variously grew and declined, all the while maintaining its pre-eminent economic and strategic role in the region. Its area was extended under the Anglo-Normans, encouraging a circuit of walls with fifteen gates and no less than twenty-three towers. A military fort, the 'Citadel' was completed in the early seventeenth century. During the Cromwellian conquest (1649-53) the city was captured by General Henry Ireton and a half-century later, following the Williamite Wars (1689-91), it was from Waterford that King James II (1633-1701) departed Ireland in political and military ruin. The changing nature of military threat eventually encouraged the dismantling of the city's walls, although significant fragments remain and can still be traced. Sections of the walls that fronted onto the quay were dismantled in 1705.

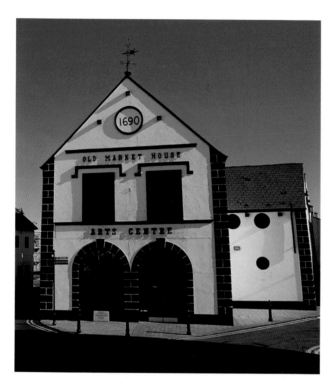

(fig. 3)
DUNGARVAN
MARKET HOUSE
Main Street
(Parnell Street),
Dungarvan
(1690)

A late seventeenth-
century market house,
now an arts centre,
forms an appealing
landmark in the medieval
core of Dungarvan.

Although largely ruinous, both circular and rectangular towers and tall stone houses remain across the county from the period before 1700; some can be dated as early as the fifteenth century. Those of circular form are sited principally along the River Suir. Several seventeenth-century fortified houses — tall stone structures, some ruined, others reconstructed — survive, mainly in west Waterford. These were mostly erected by new settlers following the Munster Plantations of the 1580s. The finest, though ruinous, examples are those at Tikincor, built for Alexander Power before 1620, and Ballyduff Castle, begun in 1627 by Andrew Tucker for the 1st Earl of Cork. The Earl had also acquired the Lismore estates, originally granted to Sir Walter Raleigh (c. 1554-1618) in the 1590s. Here he launched into an extensive and prolonged programme of building involving both the castle and the cathedral, while the town itself was developed on the site of the nucleus of the present town. The work at the castle resulted in a large new courtyarded house with ranges of two-storey buildings and towers which, as was common practice, incorporated the fabric of earlier structures. The buildings were complemented by elaborate terraced gardens and ornamental gateways. Stonemasons Nicholas and John Walsh from Waterford City were engaged to carve window frames, quoins, fireplaces, and staircases, their work reflecting the ongoing high quality of masonry in the region. What is now known as

(fig. 4)
THE RIDING HOUSE
Lismore Castle,
Lismore
(1631)

The Riding House, originally built by the 1st Earl of Cork as accommodation for a mounted guard, is one of the few surviving seventeenth-century gabled structures in Ireland.

(fig. 5)
CASTLE DODARD
Knockaungarriff
(c. 1625)

A hunting lodge, originally built for the 1st Earl of Cork in a French Chateau style, was extensively reconstructed and remodelled in the 1970s for residential use.

BALLYGUNNER CASTLE
Ballygunnercastle
(post-1640)

The fortified house expresses its medieval origins in the slight batter to the thick walls, and the carved limestone surrounds to the narrow openings.

(fig. 6)
GLENBEG HOUSE
Glen Beg
(c. 1650)

This large Jacobean house displays features characteristic of the period including projecting towers, crow-stepped gables, and stout chimney stacks. The house has been extensively restored (1999-2002).

the Riding House (1631) was built as an austere defensive gatehouse to provide accommodation for a mounted guard *(fig. 4)*. Castle Dodard (c. 1625), a small hunting lodge, was another early seventeenth-century project; it has three cylindrical corner towers with tall conical roofs and was comprehensively reconstructed in the 1970s *(fig. 5)*.

Other seventeenth-century houses of note include Mount Odell (1678) and Glenbeg

House (c. 1650), near Ballyduff. Although altered and extended over the centuries, Glenbeg's original T-plan and rectangular towers can still be discerned *(fig. 6)*. Mount Odell retains its battered walls, gabled ends, steeply pitched roof, and some slate-hung sections on the rear elevation. The stairs return on the rear elevation and chimneystacks on the gables are characteristic of seventeenth-century architecture.

The Eighteenth Century

Architectural developments gathered momentum across Waterford in the course of the eighteenth century. The comparative political stability of the period, developments in trade and husbandry, and changes in the wider European architectural taste all combined to encourage a range of new building types. The vernacular tradition that accommodated both the average domestic dwelling, and a growing array of early industrial buildings such as mills, sat side by side with a more formalised architectural idiom dominated by various interpretations of the Classical past and architectural books inspired by the Italian Renaissance. The latter taste was, in Waterford's case, filtered through developments and changes of fashion in London and Dublin, together with influences from west of England cities such as Bath and Bristol.

Existing settlements were refurbished and enhanced across the county, and some new towns were developed. Many buildings survive from this period although a few formerly isolated structures have been engulfed by later developments; this is the case at Newtown House (c. 1750), Tramore, a substantial five-bay house with enclosed porch *(fig. 7)*. An improving spirit was one of the characteristics of the age, and societies aimed at enhancing farming methods and manufacturing were not uncommon. The Dublin Society, now the Royal Dublin Society, was perhaps the most famous and was founded in 1731 for 'improving husbandry, manufacture and the useful arts and sciences'. In keeping with this aspiration Lord Grandison, a member, developed Villierstown (c. 1751) to the south of his Dromana estate as 'a new & neat colony erected; for the advancement of the Linen Manufacture'. The layout of Villierstown today has inherited elements of the original formal plan. The wide main street, flanked by plain stone buildings that would

BALLYCANVAN BIG
Spring Hill
(c. 1725)

Originally powered by a mill race channelled from Ballycanvan Stream, the ruined remains of a mill building illustrate the long standing industrial legacy of County Waterford.

(fig. 7)
NEWTOWN HOUSE
Newtown
(c. 1750)

This attractive, substantial house of solid massing is historically associated with the Power family; a wing was added in the mid twentieth century and accommodates a private chapel.

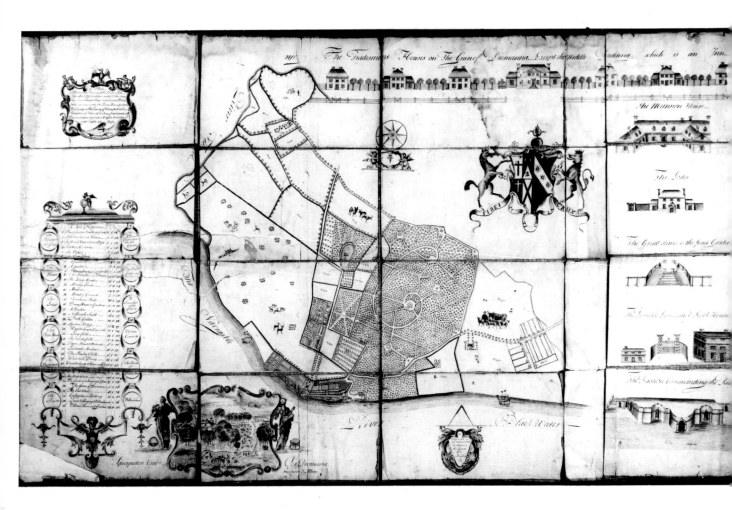

originally have been rendered, focuses on a centrally placed church (1748), which itself closes the vista from another broad street, The Green. Set behind handsome gate piers with wrought iron gates, the cruciform plan church is built of rubble stone with limestone decorative detailing, and is distinguished by a broken pediment over the entrance *(figs. 8 - 9)*.

THE DROMANA MAP (1751)

The Dromana Map shows the relationship of the Dromana estate to the planned village of Villierstown. Few of the buildings illustrated on the 'main street' are recognisable today, although a number of the structures detailed from the estate survive intact.

Courtesy of the Irish Architectural Archive.

(fig. 8)
VILLIERSTOWN CHURCH
Villierstown
(1748)

A cut-stone plaque
records the association
of Mary Villiers Stuart
with the church.

(fig. 9)
VILLIERSTOWN CHURCH
Villierstown
(1748)

Occupying a prominent
site, the church forms
the centrepiece in the
planned village of
Villierstown.

VIEW OF THE
BLACKWATER BELOW
DROMANA HOUSE
(1795-9)

An aquatint of
the Blackwater by
Thomas Sautell Roberts
(1760-1826) depicts a
Romantic landscape with
Dromana House promi-
nently positioned on an
elevated site overlooking
the river.

*Courtesy of the National
Gallery of Ireland.*

DROMANA HOUSE
Dromana
(c. 1675)

Built in the late seven-
teenth century an early
tower house was
encased by subsequent
building, and remains
discernible to this day.
The building was
enlarged in the 1780s
for Geroge Mason-Villiers
and remodelled c. 1822.
The later range was
cleared in 1966, restor-
ing the house to a form
recognisable in the
Dromana Map.

DROMANA HOUSE
Dromana

A fine cut-limestone
Gibbsian doorcase is the
sole apparent decorative
concession in the surviv-
ing house.

DROMANA HOUSE
Dromana
(c. 1750)

A formal terrace
overlooking the River
Blackwater, the platform
is formed by the roof
of a boathouse below.
The structure, known as
'The Bastions', features
as a detail on the
Dromana Map.

The ongoing development of towns and villages was complemented by the growth of a transport infrastructure that saw an improved provision of roads and bridges. The impressive low-lying eleven-arch bridge (c. 1700) at Tallowbridge, built of rubble stone, dates from early in the century *(fig. 10)*. The design of Knocklofty Bridge (c. 1770) on the upper River Suir, has been attributed to Thomas Ivory (d. 1786). Ivory was also responsible for the elegant triple arched bridge (c. 1775) over the River Blackwater at Lismore. This was constructed of rubble limestone with fine stonework detailing and segmental arches supported on slender piers. Towards the end of the century a wooden bridge (1793-4) designed by the American engineer Lemuel Cox (1736-1806) was erected across the River Suir in Waterford City on the site of the present Edmund Rice Bridge. It replaced a ferry service and encouraged links with County Kilkenny as well as later developments on the far side of the river.

(fig. 10)
TALLOW BRIDGE
Tallowbridge
(c. 1700)

A low lying bridge of rubble stone makes an attractive impression in the village of Tallowbridge, and is one of the earliest surviving bridges in County Waterford.

(fig. 11)
WATERFORD
MILITARY BARRACKS
Green Street,
Waterford
(c. 1780)

A self contained group of soldiers' homes originally formed part of an extensive complex in Waterford City. Simple Classical details contribute to the architectural value of the houses.

(fig. 12)
PLAN FOR NEW
GENEVA SETTLEMENT
(1783)

A plan, attributed to James Gandon (1743-1823) serves as a reminder of the settlement proposed for Swiss refugees in the late eighteenth century. The layout, of planned residential squares fronting on to a concave feature, suggests that the colony was intended to replace Passage East, which features a comparable arrangement to this day.

Courtesy of the Irish Architectural Archive.

Despite the 'improvements' and comparative stability of the age, unrest, political and otherwise, was never far below the surface. Barracks indicated a strong military presence across the county. The large, now restored, military barracks at Dungarvan Castle dates from early in the century. A further extensive complex (c. 1780) was erected at Ballybricken Hill, Waterford City, on a long established defensive site. Other buildings there include some three and four-bay stone cottages (c. 1780) with a separate bath house; the cottages served as accommodation for soldiers and their families *(fig. 11)*. These modest buildings have retained many of their original features such as timber sash window frames, panelled doors, and stone

surrounds. A stark, stone barracks near Crooke, known as the New Geneva Barracks (begun 1786), is all that remains of an interesting but abortive project that took place in the latter part of the century *(figs. 12 - 13)*. Following a wave of political unrest in Switzerland, Newtown was designated for Swiss settlers as

(fig. 13)
NEW GENEVA BARRACKS
Newtown
(Begun 1786)

In use until 1824, the New Geneva Barracks complex played an important role in the aftermath of the 1798 Rebellion when it was used as a detention camp. The building illustrated was subsequently converted to a farmhouse.

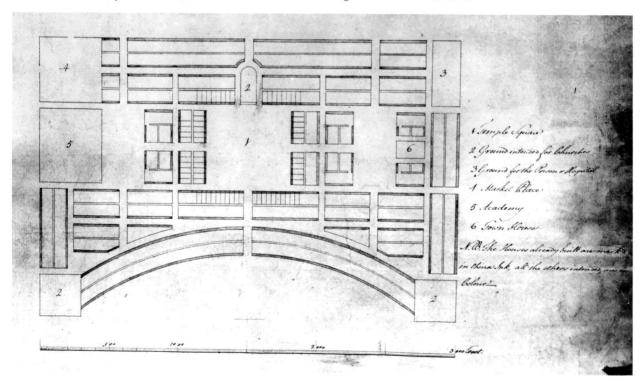

THE QUAYS, WATERFORD, 5824. W.L.

THE QUAYS
Waterford
(c. 1890)

An archival photograph illustrates the busy commercial activity along Waterford's quays, which gathered apace throughout the eighteenth century.

Courtesy of the National Library of Ireland.

'New Geneva' in an attempt to attract Protestant refugees. Advocates of the project hoped that it would encourage industry and bring 'reform' to the area. Although supported by a substantial grant from Parliament (1783), with local grandees as commissioners and significant grants of land together with plans by the eminent James Gandon (1743-1823), the initiative came to nothing. The New Geneva Barracks was used as a detention camp in the aftermath of the 1798 Rebellion but was subsequently abandoned and some of the buildings dismantled.

Waterford City, by now the second city of Ireland, was the focus of the most striking architectural growth with a quality of architectural ambition worthy of its status and aspirations. The port was a conduit for the pro-duce of much of Munster and provided access to the continent and the west of England, which in turn encouraged links with the wider world and the colonies in the Americas. The upriver development of the quay reflected the growth in the trading capacity of the port. The imposition of the Penal Laws (1691-1829), however, restricted the previous oligarchy of the rich Catholic families who had ruled the commercial life of the city. Many continued to be involved in Waterford-based business, even while domiciled on the continent. At the same time, and by way of compensating for the potential economic vacuum, the Corporation encouraged foreign traders to settle in the city, mirroring the creation of new settlements across the county.

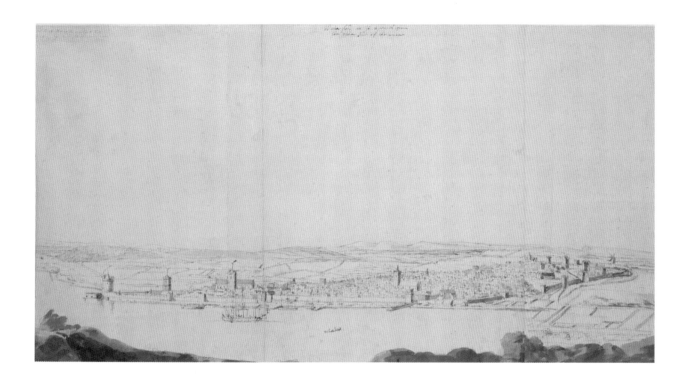

(fig. 14)
A VIEW OF WATERFORD
(c. 1699)

A depiction of Waterford by Francis Place (1647-1728) illustrates the undulating setting of the city, a characteristic that has been concealed by development and expansion over the subsequent three centuries. The city walls and windmill are primarily remembered through archival sources.

Courtesy of the National Gallery of Ireland.

Francis Place (1647-1728) depicted the city in a drawing at the turn of the century. In *A View of Waterford* (c. 1699, National Gallery of Ireland) he shows buildings packed closely together on rising ground behind walls along the river *(fig. 14)*. A large windmill is prominent on high ground. A generation later, and allowing for 'poetic licence', the Dutch born artist William van der Hagen (d. 1745), in *A View of Waterford* (1736, Waterford Town Hall), depicts a seemingly prosperous city with the open quay lined with block after block of tall buildings on the line of the demolished city walls. Charles Smith, writing in 1746, would appear to underscore the visual implications of

Van der Hagen's view. He gives detailed descriptions of some of the more important structures, praising the 'handsome private buildings' while noting that the streets and lanes remained exceedingly narrow, implying that much of the medieval street pattern remained intact at this date. In the course of time, and following the London and Dublin fashion, more spacious streets were developed, their names — George, King, Queen, and Hanover Streets — a tribute to the new Hanoverian regime (post 1714). The marshy area near Reginald's Tower was drained in the 1730s and a tree-lined Mall laid out with a bowling green located near the river. The Deanery (c. 1725) at the cathedral was built on an L-shaped plan on a corner site, incorporating some fabric from an earlier medieval building. Although extensively renovated in recent years, it forms an important component of the square *(fig. 15)*.

Smith's narrative suggests that private residences were of some splendour. The home of Alderman Samuel Barker on Great George's Street (now 5 O'Connell Street) (c. 1730) was described as 'set in large terraced gardens with statuary, ornamental canals and fountains'. The surviving house, although much altered, retains its original flight of entrance steps with decorative railings. By the middle of the century Lady Lane, one of the oldest laneways in the city, had become a fashionable residential address with many fine terraced houses of a type known as Georgian. A number of surviving examples display the characteristics of that style; usually three storeys with distinctive proportions and a decorative entrance doorcase. Number 18 Lady Lane (now Ozanam House) (c. 1750) retains an impressive stone pedimented doorcase, with original windows on the upper floor *(fig. 16)*. Others of the type survive along The Mall, a street that attracted the rich merchant class who built their homes at what was a centre of fashion and society. Although many of their houses have been refronted or altered they still retain the basic composition and scale of their original appearance. Number 30 The Mall (c. 1780) could be a townhouse of the period anywhere in these islands with the scale and compositional elements, notably a fine columned doorcase surmounted by a fanlight, characteristic of the mid-Georgian era *(fig. 17)*. The Bishop's Palace (1741-52) is the most substantial private house in the Classical style on The Mall, and just one in a series of similarly

grand ecclesiastical Church of Ireland residences built across Ireland at this time. Bishop Milles originally commissioned the building in the 1730s from the Bristol based architect and publisher of pattern books William Halfpenny, alias Michael Hoare (fl. 1723-55). Richard Castle (c. 1695-1751) adapted Halfpenny's plans in 1741 and created the massive residence to recall, in scale at least, his design for Leinster House (1741-51), Dublin. Like the Dublin work, the palace has two principal façades: one facing The Mall and the other the cathedral. Each front is characterised by finely cut ashlar limestone. Central visual emphasis is achieved through the grouping of windows, the placement of pediments, and other classical details such as niches *(fig. 18)*.

(fig. 15)
THE DEANERY
Cathedral Square/
Bailey's New Street,
Waterford
(c. 1725)

The Deanery, a well composed Georgian house, is an attractive element of Cathedral Square. The building incorporates the fabric of a medieval undercroft (c. 1468) at basement level.

(fig. 16)
OZANAM HOUSE
18 Lady Lane,
Waterford
(c. 1750)

Large Georgian houses illustrate the development of fashionable residential areas in Waterford in the mid eighteenth century. Number 18 Lady Lane incorporates fine delicate plasterwork to the interior.

(fig. 18)
WATERFORD
BISHOP'S PALACE
The Mall,
Waterford
(1741-52)

William Halfpenny,
alias Michael Hoare
(fl. 1723-55), was origi-
nally commissioned to
design the bishop's
palace but was succeed-
ed by Richard Castle
(c. 1695-1751). The
palace was completed by
John Roberts (1712-96)
and now accommodates
the Waterford City
Council offices.

(fig. 17)
30 THE MALL
Waterford
(c. 1780)

A group of houses on The
Mall incorporate features
comparable with the
Georgian squares in Dublin,
including construction in red
brick, and ornate Classical
doorcases. The rendered
embellishments to Number
30 were added in the late
nineteenth century.

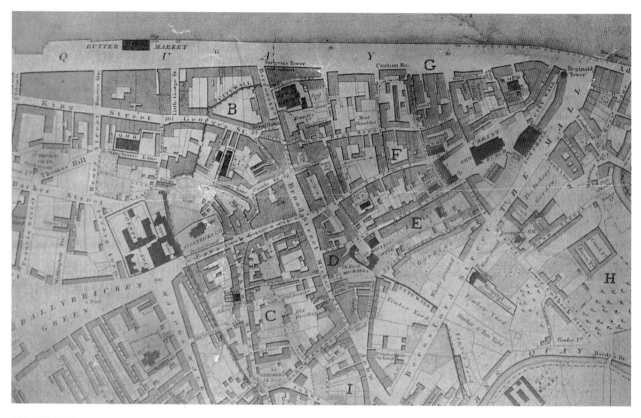

MAP OF THE CITY
OF WATERFORD AND
ITS ENVIRONS
(1834)

A map of Waterford City
by P. Leahy, dated 1834,
indicates the development
of The Mall, including the
position of Castle's
Bishop's Palace, and
Roberts' Assembly Rooms
and cathedrals.

© *Waterford City Archives.*

Many new churches were erected or reconstructed; most prominently those of the established church, the Church of Ireland. Standing in its own grounds, Saint Patrick's (1727) was built of local red sandstone with limestone dressing to its round-headed windows. It is a 'single-cell' church and has a simple pitched roof. A stone bellcote animates its western front while the interior retains many contemporary features including a timber gallery, some decorative plasterwork, and attractive leaded windows. The church is now used by the Methodist and Presbyterian communities. A comparably simple church, off Jenkin's Lane and also dedicated to Saint Patrick (1764), was built for the Roman Catholic community. This is a relatively early date for such a church in Ireland and a rare example, although few records, visual or otherwise, survive of those that did exist. The simple rectangular building had an understated exterior, which has since been altered, in contrast to the once rich interior, described by Smith as 'finely adorned with paintings...the panels of the wainscots carved and gilded'. Today the barrel-vaulted interior, with rare surviving balustraded galleries, is plain but pleasing.

The scale and ambition of development in Waterford City was matched by a comparable architectural achievement at the country seats of the greater nobility and landed gentry. As families assumed either greater political clout or greater financial power they were better placed to develop properties that reflected on their standing in society. Despite this trend some formerly important centres, notably Lismore Castle, went into a period of marked decline. Smith illustrates the castle in a semi-derelict state. In contrast, the great estate at Curraghmore House, near Portlaw, flourished *(fig. 19)*. The house was rebuilt (c. 1755), incorporating fabric of earlier houses (1654 and 1700), the interior was remodelled (c. 1785),

(fig. 19)
CURRAGHMORE HOUSE
Curraghmore
(c. 1755)

Rebuilt in the mid eighteenth century, Curraghmore House incorporates a medieval tower house (pre-1654). Interiors by James Wyatt (1747-1813) and subsequent improvements up to the late nineteenth century have come together to make it one of the finest country houses in Ireland.

Courtesy of the National Library of Ireland.

and the house extensively renovated (c. 1875). Catherine Power (d. 1769) initiated the redevelopments at the site but it was her son George De La Poer (Beresford), 1st Marquess of Waterford (1735-1800), who instigated the most dramatic phase. The house is approached by an impressive forecourt of stable ranges, some 550 feet in length, and supporting rich Classical detailing *(fig. 20)*. These ranges have been attributed to the Waterford architect John Roberts (1712-96). The interior, in common with many great houses, envelops the original medieval tower, and retains stuccowork by the Lafranchini brothers Paolo (1695-1770) and Filippo (1702-79), both of whom worked in Ireland in the 1750s. The Flemish artist Peter de Gree (1751-89) was responsible for grisaille panels; these are comparatively rare features in Ireland although there were other examples in the county by Van der Hagen. Eventually, in the 1780s, the 1st Marquess engaged the London based architect James Wyatt (1747-1813) to create a range of new rooms in the by then very fashionable neo-Classical style, characterised by a finesse of detailing and attention to archaeological precedent. The work at Curraghmore is on a par with, indeed may even surpass, work carried out by Wyatt elsewhere in Ireland at Westport House, County Mayo, and Castlecoole, County Fermanagh.

During the second half of the century Waterford City continued to grow and prosper. Its port not only channelled exports but also became increasingly important as a centre for provisioning ships. Trade and shipping fleets stopped at the port on their way between England, southern Spain, and Newfoundland, where links with Waterford became increasingly strong. The prosperity was reflected in architecture and famously in the decorative arts, most notably the making of Waterford's celebrated glass, a business initiated originally by the Penrose family. The medieval fabric of the city continued to be demolished or altered to allow for the building of new and more spacious properties. A programme of street widening that further obliterated the medieval city core was launched under the Wide Streets Commissioners.

(fig. 21)
CHRIST CHURCH
CATHEDRAL
Cathedral Square,
Waterford
(1773-9)

Historic sources record
considerable opposition
to the replacement of
the thirteenth-century
Gothic cathedral on site,
and yet Roberts's cathe-
dral now forms one of
the most important fea-
tures of the architectural
heritage of Waterford.
Evidence of the prede-
cessor survives in the
form of a truncated
Norman pillar.

(fig. 22)
CHRIST CHURCH
CATHEDRAL
Cathedral Square,
Waterford

A present day depiction
of the recently restored
cathedral illustrates
that the interior is little
changed, with the excep-
tion of the loss of the galleries; these were removed
in 1891 and the fixed box
pews were replaced with
loose seating.

INSIDE of the CATHEDRAL of CHRIST-CHURCH, WATERFORD.

(fig. 23)
CHRIST CHURCH
CATHEDRAL
Cathedral Square,
Waterford

An engraving of the
interior of the cathedral
dates from shortly after
the completion of
construction.

*Courtesy of the Irish
Architectural Archive.*

(fig. 24)
CHRIST CHURCH
CATHEDRAL
Cathedral Square,
Waterford

A cut-stone mausoleum
bears witness to the
presence of an earlier
cathedral on site.

(fig. 25)
CATHOLIC CATHEDRAL
OF THE HOLY TRINITY
Barronstrand Street,
Waterford
(1793-9)

The Catholic cathedral features an internal arrangement comparable with that of Christ Church Cathedral and bears witness to a common design source. An ornate interior, in which the galleries are retained, provided a foil to the severe external treatment of a building that was originally concealed from view off Barronstrand Street.

In this period the city not only attracted leading architects, notably James Gandon, but also fostered its own accomplished designers, particularly the Roberts family, of whom Thomas Roberts and his son John are the most distinguished. John's most prestigious buildings were cathedrals, one for the Church of Ireland and the other Roman Catholic. That two cathedrals of different denominations shared an architect, not to mention that a Catholic church on this scale was built at all in this period, reflects favourably on the tolerant spirit of the county and city. The Church of Ireland Cathedral (1773-9), Christ Church, is the more prominent *(fig. 21)*. It adjoins the bishop's palace, and stands on the site of the former churchyard of an earlier cathedral in Cathedral Square. It seems that Halfpenny had also provided plans (London: RIBA) for the cathedral — a further indication of links between Waterford and Bristol in these years. The comparatively austere exterior is relieved by a mon-umental Tuscan portico while a striking polygonal spire forms a prominent feature of the Waterford skyline to this day. The recently restored interior has been altered over the centuries but still retains its late eighteenth-century impact exuding a light-filled airiness, the overall effect embellished with delicate ceiling plasterwork (1818) *(figs. 22 - 24)*. The façade of Roberts's Catholic Cathedral of the Holy Trinity (1793-9) dates from 1893-97. The cathedral originally had no street presence and the interior must have appeared all the more surprising in consequence *(fig. 25)*. While compromised by later well-intentioned interventions it is nonetheless impressive, suggesting, if on a smaller scale, a great Roman church with groin vaults resting on a forest of slender Corinthian columns. The columns are given added height through supporting blocks of stone, known as dosserets, from which the vaults appear to spring.

(fig. 26)
WATERFORD
TOWN HALL AND
THEATRE ROYAL
The Mall,
Waterford
(1783)

John Roberts's proposal
for a civic building suc-
cessfully combined
assembly rooms and a
playhouse in an integrat-
ed scheme; the building
presents a frontage of
Classical symmetry on to
The Mall.

(fig. 27)
WATERFORD
TOWN HALL AND
THEATRE ROYAL
The Mall,
Waterford

Fine carved limestone
detailing enlivens the
exterior of the building.

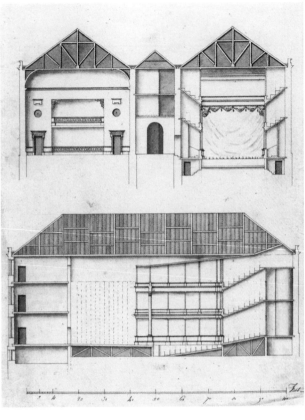

(fig. 28)
WATERFORD
TOWN HALL AND
THEATRE ROYAL
The Mall,
Waterford

An unidentified drawing
of the internal elevation
and cross section of an
assembly rooms and
playhouse complex cor-
responds comparatively
with the form and
arrangement of Robert's
scheme in Waterford.

*Courtesy of the Irish
Architectural Archive.*

Roberts also designed the nearby Assembly Rooms and Play House, now serving as Waterford Town Hall and Theatre Royal (1783) *(figs. 26 - 28)*. A prominently scaled building on The Mall, it echoed the contemporary and architecturally distinguished assembly rooms in cities like Dublin, Bath, Bristol, and York. The Assembly Rooms in Waterford were inevitably designed according to the Classical taste of the period, with the diverse interior arrangements fronted by a regularly balanced Classical façade. The small intimate auditorium of the theatre was remodelled in 1876 in a manner redolent of current fashion, with a Gothic quality recalling the Gaiety Theatre, London (1868) and the original appearance of the Gaiety Theatre, Dublin (1871) *(figs. 29 - 30)*. In its scale and detailing it has been compared to the first Shakespeare Memorial Theatre (1877), Stratford-on-Avon, designed by architects

(fig. 29)
WATERFORD
TOWN HALL AND
THEATRE ROYAL
The Mall,
Waterford

Remodelled in 1876
in the Gothic style, the
auditorium of the theatre
comprises three tiers; the
dress circle and upper
circle are supported by
cast-iron pillars. The hier-
archy of the Victorian
class system could be
measured by the discrep-
ancy in the prices
charged for seats on
each level.

(fig. 30)
WATERFORD
TOWN HALL AND
THEATRE ROYAL
The Mall,
Waterford

A view of the dress circle
and upper circle shows
pointed arches and pen-
dentives supporting a
shallow 'saucer' dome.

(fig. 31)
WATERFORD CHAMBER
OF COMMERCE
(MORRIS HOUSE)
2 Great George's Street,
Waterford
(c. 1785)

An imposing, Classical-
style townhouse built for
William Morris to the
designs of John Roberts.
The embellishments to
the façade were added
in the late nineteenth
century. The house
makes a strong impres-
sion on the vista through
Gladstone Street from
the quays.

(fig. 32)
WATERFORD CHAMBER
OF COMMERCE
(MORRIS HOUSE)
2 Great George's Street,
Waterford

An elegant cantilevered
oval spiral staircase
was inserted by the
Waterford Chamber of
Commerce in 1830.
The stairwell is sur-
mounted by a delicate
glazed dome sitting in
a rich plasterwork frame.

*Courtesy of the Irish
Architectural Archive.*

Dogdshun and Unsworth. A few years later, Roberts designed the imposing Morris House (c. 1785), Great George's Street, for the rich merchant William Morris of Rosduff *(fig. 31)*. It was purchased a generation later for a fraction of its initial building cost by the future Waterford Chamber of Commerce who undertook internal alterations in 1830, including the oval dome above the spectacularly elegant cantilevered staircase *(fig. 32)*. Although later embellishments to the façade are not part of Robert's original scheme, his grand composition, a four-storey house with a wide fanlit columned entrance doorway, rivals anything to be found in Irish domestic architecture of the time.

The Nineteenth Century

The major political upheavals across Europe at the end of the eighteenth century were not without dramatic impact in Ireland, most notably in the 1798 Rebellion and its bloody aftermath, and the Act of Union (1800). Despite such turmoil, Waterford enjoyed a period of expansion during the first decades of the new century. Ongoing mercantile and business success encouraged urban developments across the county; new towns were planned and existing towns enhanced. Industrial and agricultural innovation and eventually new modes of transport all brought change. Yet there were inevitable economic downturns, all of which had consequences for towns and villages across the county. Agricultural production was threatened by the hard times that followed the cessation of the Napoleonic Wars (1803-15), and the catastrophic Great Famine (1845-50) impacted the entire county. Social changes, notably Catholic Emancipation (1829) and the subsequent empowering of Catholicism encouraged a wave of church building. New churches were accompanied by associated buildings, including schools and convents. The Church of Ireland similarly embarked on an extensive building campaign funded by the Board of First Fruits (fl. c. 1711-1833), an administrative body for annual government funding to the established church.

The development of infrastructure, mostly as private initiatives, was a characteristic of much of the century. Canals were utilised, navigable rivers further exploited for use in the transport of goods, and railways arrived with a whole array of new architectural forms. A canal linking Cappoquin to the River Blackwater was completed around 1814, allowing the town to act as an important transport hub with steam packet links to Fermoy and Youghal in County Cork *(fig. 33)*.

Waterford merchants had been putting the Westminster government under prolonged pressure to improve postal services between Ireland and England. In the 1820s a new harbour was finally developed at Dunmore East, originally a small fishing village. Until superseded by Dunmore East, Cheekpoint, at the mouth of the Suir estuary had been the port for the packet boat service to and from England. The handsome red brick Daisybank House (c. 1765) probably served as a hotel in the town's heyday *(fig. 34)*. Work on the new pier and harbour (1814-41) was carried out over a long period; four steamers were employed on the route to and from Milford Haven *(fig. 35)*. Dunmore Harbour House (c. 1820) was built to accommodate travellers *(fig. 36)*. Waterford's maritime importance was reflected not only in its harbour improvements but also in the lighthouse developments along its coast. The distinctive lighthouse (c. 1824) at the end of the pier in Dunmore East joined a garland of lighthouses constructed around the

(fig. 33)
CAPPOQUIN
AND LISMORE
(1814)

The Duke of Devonshire developed a canal to link Cappoquin with Lismore. Although its commercial success was sporadic, the canal gave rise to related structures such as the bridge at Ballyrafter Flats.

CAPPOQUIN
(c. 1890)

A view of a steampacket ship, a feature historically associated with the development of the canal at Cappoquin. The Cappoquin Railway Viaduct (opened 1878) is visible in the background.

Courtesy of the National Library of Ireland.

(fig. 34)
DAISYBANK HOUSE
Cheekpoint
(c. 1765)

A lofty red brick house dominates the small fishing village of Cheekpoint. The house once operated as a hotel and, as illegal smuggling was a prolific activity at the time, was possibly intended to be a constabulary barracks.

(fig. 35)
DUNMORE EAST
HARBOUR
Dunmore Bay,
Dunmore East
(1814)

The pier, designed by
Alexander Nimmo (1783-
1832), was intended to
shelter a harbour which,
originally developed as a
steampacket port linked
with Milford Haven, has
supported much of the
economy of Dunmore
East ever since.

(fig. 36)
DUNMORE
HARBOUR HOUSE
Dock Road,
Dunmore East
(c. 1820)

A building with a convoluted history, Dunmore
Harbour House was originally built as a seaside
residence for the Marquis
of Waterford, but
became a hotel shortly
after. Subsequently in
use as a convent, the
house served as a hotel
in the latter part of the
twentieth century and is
now uninhabited.

*Courtesy of the National
Library of Ireland.*

(fig. 37)
DUNMORE EAST
LIGHTHOUSE
Dunmore Bay,
Dunmore East
(1824)

Forming an integral part
of the development of
the harbour as envisaged
by Alexander Nimmo,
the lighthouse presented
as a fluted Doric column,
the lantern substituting
for a capital. The carved
detailing to the granite
stone work is indicative
of exceptional stone
masonry.

coast of Ireland in these years. It was built in
the form of a giant fluted Doric column to a
design by the engineer Alexander Nimmo
(1783-1832) **(fig. 37)**. Nimmo has also been
attributed with the equally distinctive and well
known 'Metal Man' (1819) on Great Newtown
Head near Tramore, an unlit beacon or pointer used to guide ships **(figs. 38 - 41)**. The cast-
iron figure wearing a sailor's uniform stands
atop a stone pillar, and points out to sea.
Other navigational support structures include
the small crenellated tower (c. 1800) with an

METAL MAN.TRAMORE.Co.WATERFORD.9054.W.L.

(fig. 38)
THE METAL
MAN TOWER
Westtown
(1819)

Attributed to Alexander Nimmo, The Metal Man Tower formed part of a group of unlit beacons positioned on the headlands flanking the notoriously treacherous Tramore Bay. An element of the folklore of the county is illustrated in this archival image depicting a group of single women hopping in a ring around the tower in the hope of finding a husband.

Courtesy of the National Library of Ireland.

(fig. 39)
THE METAL
MAIN TOWER
Westtown

The profile of the tapered towers elegantly punctuates the landscape.

(fig. 40)
THE METAL
MAN TOWER
Westtown

The brightly painted cast-iron figure in a sailor's uniform points out to sea, warning mariners of the dangers of the rocky Tramore Bay.

(fig. 41)
THE METAL
MAN TOWER
Westtown

A collection of three slender towers overlooking the Atlantic Ocean produces a dramatic silhouette.

external staircase on Ardmore Head *(fig. 42)*. Mine Head Lighthouse (1851), also at Ardmore, was built for what became the regulatory body for lighthouses around the coast, the Commissioners for Irish Lights *(fig. 43)*. It typifies the fusion of engineering excellence and simple refined aesthetic that marks such schemes. It is built of quality tooled granite ashlar and stands eighty-seven feet high on a dramatic promontory. The usual ancillary buildings, including two keeper's houses, are set within an adjoining enclosure.

Land transport needs ensured that bridges and roads were strengthened or newly built in response to increased usage. Not only did such bridges facilitate communication but, as at Ferrybank, they could encourage a spate of pri-

(fig. 42)
ARDMORE HEAD
WATCH TOWER
Dysert
(c. 1800)

The small scale observation tower was possibly associated with the Napoleonic defences. Simple Gothic-style dressings, including battlemented parapets, lend a picturesque quality to the composition.

(fig. 43)
MINE HEAD
LIGHTHOUSE
Monagoush
(1851)

Built as part of a nationwide programme sponsored by the Commissioners of Irish Lights, the lighthouse is an appealing feature on Mine Head. Fine tooling to the granite produces a subtle textured effect in the granite ashlar stone work.

vate and commercial development by opening up areas previously difficult to access. Metal milestones, cast by H.C. Price and Company, Bristol, survive in the region around Lismore and Cappoquin *(fig. 44)*.

Infrastructural developments by the Devonshire and Beresford Estates in towns such as Dungarvan were frequently motivated by political expediency. That Tallow lost its borough status in 1801 may have precluded it from improvements in subsequent years. Political expediency or not, such interventions had a lasting architectural legacy. The building of a bridge over the River Colligan in Dungarvan was part of a wider improvement of the Devonshire interests in the town, which had previously been in decline. William Atkinson (c. 1773-1839), architect to the 6th Duke, designed the Causeway Bridge (1816), with the work supervised by Jesse Hartley (1780-1860). The handsome rusticated sandstone bridge, with massive voussoirs and scroll keystones, linked the town with the fishing village of Abbeyside *(fig. 45)*. The nearby Barnawee Bridge (c. 1815) was built in a comparable style. A five-arched bridge (c. 1847) in Cappoquin was begun as a famine relief work scheme, and replaced an earlier wooden bridge.

(fig. 44)
RED FORGE CROSSROADS
Garryduff
(c. 1850)

This cast-iron milestone is one of a group characteristic of County Waterford and cast by the H.C. Price Company, Bristol. Similar milestones on the main Dungarvan road are set into stone depots, illustrating the formalisation of the county's road network in the mid nineteenth century.

(fig. 45)
CAUSEWAY BRIDGE
Dungarvan
(1816)

A handsome bridge sponsored by the Duke of Devonshire links Dungarvan with Abbeyside over the Colligan River estuary. The bridge incorporates fine Runcorn (Cheshire) sandstone and is distinguished by the heavy rustication to the elongated voussoirs.

Courtesy of the National Library of Ireland.

At Lismore, the magnificent seven-arched Cavendish Bridge (1858) incorporates some of the fabric from an earlier bridge (1774-9). It is constructed of broken coursed limestone with round-headed niches on the south face; the tooled limestone parapets have cut-stone coping with decorative iron lamp standards *(fig. 46)*. By contrast the cast-iron bridge (1887), Ballyduff, makes few concessions to past traditions. Instead it proclaims its industrial origins and materials in a logical but elegant manner *(fig. 47)*. The bridge was constructed by E.C. and J. Keay to the designs of W.E. L'Estrange Duffin (1843-1925), the Waterford County Engineer.

The effect of improved road and water transport was greatly overshadowed by the advent of the railways. As elsewhere across the world they transformed concepts of speed and travel, and allowed for the movement of people and goods as never before. Railway projects provided an array of engineering works: cuttings, embankments, bridges, viaducts, and stations; all of which left an impact on the architectural heritage of the county as well as promoting growth and development. By 1853 the Waterford and Kilkenny Railway reached as far as Dunkitt, just outside the city of Waterford, with a line to Limerick completed in the same year. The discovery of seaside holidays was one of the social phenomena of the age, and the coastal town of Tramore, situated on a beautiful bay, quickly became a resort following the opening a railway line in 1853. The line was closed in the early 1960s and the surviving disused station (1853) provides a visual echo of its past. By the 1870s the Waterford, Dungarvan, and Lismore Railway provided links across the county. The extension of the Great Southern and Western line to Lismore resulted in a number of purpose built structures, including a train shed and a station house (both 1872) constructed of imported Derbyshire grit stone quarried on the Duke of Devonshire's English estates. Both buildings were designed in a neo-Tudor style, a picturesque approach not uncommon in railway related architecture. The engineering component of the Lismore extension includes the Ballyvoyle Tunnel (1878) and two viaducts

(fig. 46)
CAVENDISH BRIDGE
(LISMORE BRIDGE)
Lismore
(1858)

An elegant Classically-detailed bridge, built by C.H. Hunt and E.P. Nagle to the designs of Charles Tarrant (1815-77), County Surveyor of Waterford, and sponsored by the Duke of Devonshire, incorporates the fabric of an earlier bridge (1774-9).

(fig. 47)
BALLYDUFF BRIDGE
Ballyduff
(1887)

Designed by W.E. L'Estrange Duffin (1843-1925), Waterford County Engineer, the bridge at Ballyduff made use of the latest technological advances and remains one of the finest iron bridges in the county. The lattice parapets are a distinctive characteristic of the design and produce an attractive rhythmic visual effect.

(fig. 48)
MAHON RAILWAY
VIADUCT
Kilmacthomas
(1878)

A graceful viaduct of
eight arches was built as
part of the Fishguard and
Rosslare Railways &
Harbours Company devel-
opment of the Great
Southern Railway line in
County Waterford. The
viaduct dominates its sur-
roundings and poses an
artificial horizon in the
centre of Kilmacthomas.

(fig. 49)
CAPPOQUIN RAILWAY
STATION
Cook Street (off),
Cappoquin
(1878)

Following the closure
of the line in 1967, the
station at Cappoquin was
converted to residential
use without compromis-
ing the historic integrity
of the composition. The
contemporary railway
station at Lismore is
built in a similar style.

(1878), together with a modest station in Kilmacthomas (1878). The eight-arch Mahon Railway Viaduct (1878) designed by James Otway (1843-1906) and built by Smith Finlayson and Company of Glasgow, forms a prominent landmark that dominates the town of Kilmacthomas *(fig. 48)*. It is a good example of the high level of expertise in technical work, engineering, and stone-masonry practiced in railway construction. The Station House (1878), Cappoquin, was adapted to private use when the station shut down in 1967 *(fig. 49)*. Several features have been retained, however, including the platform canopy supported on three cast-iron columns with floral motif capitals. The original goods and water tower (both c. 1880) also survive. The platform itself now serves as a fine terrace overlooking a sunken garden, and the timber signal hut (c. 1925) has its decorative bargeboards still intact.

BALLYVOYLE
RAILWAY VIADUCT
Ballyvoyle/
Knockyoolahan East
(1923)

Originally opened as part
of the development of the
Great Southern Railway
line in 1878, the viaduct
pictured was built in 1923
following the destruction
of an earlier model during
'The Troubles' (1922-3).
The cast-iron spans on
mass concrete pylon piers
terminate at either end
with stone abutments sur-
viving from the original
scheme. The viaduct was
closed in 1982.

*Courtesy of the National
Library of Ireland.*

TRAMORE
(c. 1890)

The railway station com-
plex pictured in the foreground was in many ways
responsible for the expansion of Tramore as a fashionable seaside resort
throughout the nine-
teenth century. Villas and
terraces of houses were
strategically planned to
capitalise on the pictur-
esque coastal vistas.

*Courtesy of the National
Library of Ireland.*

Many Waterford towns, some of which had suffered neglect, experienced growth throughout the century. Dungarvan's relative importance as a port had declined over the years and the town was quite dilapidated by the late eighteenth century. However, beginning around 1801, the Devonshire Estate laid out the regular plan and streetscape still discernable to this day. The planning was on a grand scale, evoking metropolitan aspirations, with elements that recalled the formal streetscapes of contemporary London and Dublin. It stands in contrast to the medieval street pattern further east. Later, between 1825 and 1827, the Beresford Estate erected new housing to the west of the town. New reservoirs ensured a clean supply of drinking water, and the development of the town as a centre for fisheries further alleviated previous decline. Lismore also benefited from urban improvements; the addition of the impressively wide Main and West Streets, as in Dungarvan, indicated a sense of grand urban-style planning, or at least inspiration. Street furniture with a social benefit enhanced the overall effect. The Ambrose Power Memorial public drinking fountain (1872), built at the junction of these streets in memory of the former Archdeacon of Lismore, is a prime example *(fig. 50)*. Water pumps became more commonplace across the county. That on The Green at Villierstown (c. 1875) is of a distinctive octagonal shape with Gothic tracery detailing *(fig. 52)*. In Lismore, during the 1820s and 1830s, fifty-five cottages were erected for estate workers on New Street and Chapel Lane. This was the first significant development outside the limits of the ancient medieval enclosures of the town. Although recently renovated, a terraced house in New

Street (c. 1825) has retained original decorative features such as dormer windows and bargeboards *(fig. 51)*. The distinctive early windows also survive. These are of a horizontal sash type, a feature once common to Lismore and its locality. Larger detached two-storey houses (c. 1822-7) were erected on South Mall. Many, adding greatly to the charm of the town, retain original features and materials such as timber framed windows.

(fig. 50)
AMBROSE POWER
MEMORIAL FOUNTAIN
The Square,
Lismore
(1872)

Erected to commemorate Archdeacon Ambrose Power, the fountain occupies a prominent site in the centre of Lismore. The vigorous carved detailing is evidence of high quality stone masonry and craftsmanship.

GRATTAN SQUARE
Dungarvan
(c. 1890)

A formal square, laid out by the Devonshire estate as Market Square in 1801, shows buildings of common proportions and uniform height producing a harmonious streetscape. Two taller buildings originally formed a 'gateway' opening on to Meagher Street.

Courtesy of the National Library of Ireland.

(fig. 51)
NEW STREET
Lismore
(c. 1825)

One of a terrace of houses intended for use by workers on the Lismore Castle estate, this unit has been extensively remodelled to produce the present appearance. The horizontal sash windows to the dormer attic are characteristic of the area, and may have been introduced by carpenters imported from the Duke of Devonshire's English estates.

THE SQUARE
Lismore
(post-1902)

An archival view of
The Square illustrates
the important anchor
sites in the centre of
the town including the
Lismore Arms Hotel,
the RedHouse Inn, the
Courthouse, and the
Ambrose Power
Memorial fountain occu-
pying an important posi-
tion at the junction of
three streets.

*Courtesy of the National
Library of Ireland.*

LISMORE
(c. 1955)

An aerial view of Lismore
illustrates the expansion
of the town beyond the
confines of the medieval
ecclesiastical core. The
New Street and Chapel
Lane development of the
1820s and 1830s is
apparent at the bottom,
while South Mall (1822-7)
is depicted in the centre
of the image.

*Courtesy of the National
Library of Ireland.*

(fig. 52)
THE GREEN
Villierstown
(c. 1875)

A waterpump belonging
to a rare design group
includes bas-relief Gothic-
style tracery on a pan-
elled octagonal shaft.

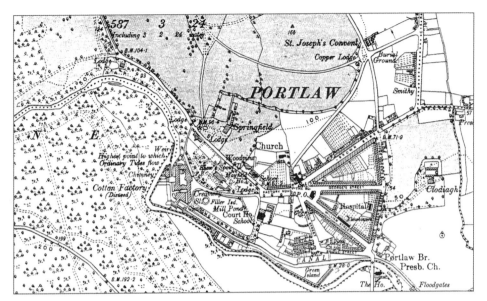

PORTLAW
(1903)

The Ordnance Survey 1903 edition highlights the radial plan that formed the centre of the 'Model' village, the cotton factory complex, and the Malcomson estates on the outskirts.

Courtesy of Trinity College Dublin.

In the 1820s a 'Model' village was developed at Portlaw to house workers for the successful local cotton manufactory, which had been set up by the Malcomson family on the banks of the Clodiagh River. In scale and planning the village may be compared with contemporary 'Model' towns developed around industrial centres in England, Scotland, and the United States of America. In the 1850s and 1860s, under Joseph Malcomson, the village was redesigned entailing the use of formal planning principles. Regularly planned wide streets with uniform house frontages and straight axes radiated from a central open space known as the Square. Workers' accommodation comprised fifty two-storey and more than 250 single-storey houses of a uniform pattern. The houses provided a standard of construction and comfort then comparatively rare. Kitchens had cooking ranges and piped hot water while the airy rooms had individual fireplaces. The exterior walls were of lime-rendered stone and each house was surmounted by a distinctive roof type known as a 'Portlaw roof', a type developed by the Malcomsons to be both efficient and cost effective. Layers of tarred calico were stretched on curved trellised softwood frames to form a weatherproof covering. Substantial overhanging eaves also characterised the roof type, found elsewhere in Waterford and nearby at Carrick-on-Suir, County Tipperary.

THE SQUARE
Portlaw
(c. 1890)

Three wide streets, Brown Street, George's Street, and William Street form a radial plan and meet at The Square. The buildings illustrated comprised the commercial centre of the village and once included a hotel.

Courtesy of the National Library of Ireland.

(fig. 53)
DOCK ROAD
Dunmore East
(c. 1840)

Two terraces of purpose-
built thatched holiday
cottages flank Dock Road
as it leads to the harbour
area of Dunmore East.
The terraces contribute
considerably to the char-
acter of the townscape.

While improved transport, and occasionally
industry, encouraged the growth of towns, other factors also encouraged urban development
in the Waterford region, including the rise of
sea bathing as a fashionable activity. As
Tramore opened up to holidaymakers and day-
trippers with the advent of the railway, this in
turn led to the building of holiday homes and
terraces of houses providing accommodation
for visitors. At Dunmore East substantial holiday homes, in the form of purpose built
thatched cottages (c. 1840), were erected
for rent *(fig. 53)*. While some have been
demolished others have been extended and still
add to the picturesque nature of the town,
which combines a holiday ambience with the
more utilitarian aspect of a working harbour.
The resort setting also encouraged the building
of more extensive properties, such as the prominently sited Villa Marina (1864) designed by
John Skipton Mulvany (1813-71) for David
Malcomson of Portlaw. Now a hotel, it retains

DUNMORE EAST
(c. 1890)

Dunmore East experi-
enced part of the boom
development of coastal
villages as seaside resorts
in the Victorian period
and included a number of
thatched holiday homes.

Only a small number of
the houses survive intact
to this day.

*Courtesy of the National
Library of Ireland.*

large rounded bays and a distinctive roofline *(fig. 54)*. Early hotels were erected in Lismore (1846) *(fig. 55)* and Cappoquin, the role of the latter town as a transport hub resulted in the construction of several small-scale hotels including the former Moore's Hotel (c. 1870) *(fig. 56)*.

Despite its fluctuating economy Waterford City continued to grow, even more so in times of poverty as growing numbers of the homeless moved in from the countryside in search of work. In due course much of its eighteenth-century appearance would be altered, with shopfronts added to earlier buildings, or completely new buildings erected in the latest fashion. Fine domestic architecture initially retained the forms favoured by the eighteenth

century. King's Terrace on the lower part of Saint Thomas's Hill is typical. Number 3 King's Terrace (c. 1820) is one of five three-storey houses situated in this small enclave, originally a cul-de-sac; the house retains its original glazing and decorative fan-lit doorway. Smaller towns and villages across the county assumed their essential urban characteristics during this period, and some remain little altered. All along the coast, from Tramore to Dungarvan, there are several small villages such as Annestown that are little changed. Substantial houses in other villages, such as those in Barrack Street (c. 1830), Passage East, indicate a previous, albeit brief, period of prosperity.

(fig. 54)
HAVEN HOTEL
(VILLA MARINA)
Dock Road,
Dunmore East
(1864)

Built as the seaside holiday home of the Malcomson family, the villa shares stylistic characteristics with their properties in Portlaw, including the bow-ended flanking wings that are a feature of Woodlock and Mayfield House.

(fig. 55)
LISMORE ARMS HOTEL
Main Street/The Square,
Lismore
(1846)

Established on the site of an earlier building, the hotel is one of the earliest surviving purpose-built commercial properties in Lismore. The hotel is noted for its historic associations with the author William M. Thackeray (1811-63).

(fig. 56)
MOORE'S HOTEL
Main Street,
Cappoquin
(c. 1870)

Although no longer serving its original purpose, the hotel building survives as evidence of the continued commercialisation of Cappoquin in the latter half of the nineteenth century.

(fig. 57)
PORTLAW COURTHOUSE
AND SCHOOL
Factory Road (off),
Portlaw
(c. 1850)

A fine Classical-style building successfully combines
the civic elements of the
planned 'Model' village of
Portlaw in an integrated
design. The courthouse
central block is framed by
two classroom ranges.

The administration of justice and the enforcement of law and order resulted in the construction of an array of courthouses and barracks, many of which continue to serve their original purpose. As a rule, courthouses were erected in the Classical style, which was perceived as appropriate to the spirit of justice. The mid-century courthouse (c. 1850) in Portlaw, which also housed a school, incorporated details such as pilasters, frieze, and cornice *(fig. 57)*. In spite of its dignified exterior, the stone parapet fronted an economically built 'Portlaw roof.' Lismore Courthouse (1815), now a heritage centre, occupied a prominent street corner. Stone-built in the Classical style with a central pedimented break-front flanked by two side bays, it is surmounted by a small clock tower that emphasises its landmark role in the streetscape. The court-house (1830) on what is now Meagher Street, Dungarvan, is similarly prominent. It is built in a reduced version of the Classical style, as pronounced in the scale and composition as it is in the detailing, with Classical elements reduced to basics such as shallow pilasters and a plain cornice. The building benefits from fine ashlar limestone work. The courthouse (1849) in Waterford City is, by way of contrast, far more robust in its Classical massing *(figs. 58 - 59)*. It stands to the east of the old city, indicating the drift of its expansion by the middle of the century, and replaced a distinguished courthouse designed by James Gandon, which has been the subject of much study. The new courthouse, designed by John B. Keane (d. 1859), benefits greatly from an open site that allows its impressive giant pedimented Ionic portico to be appreciated from a distance. It suggests a swagger and confidence belying the recent cataclysmic famine, and the growing political and social instability of the time.

(fig. 58)
WATERFORD CITY
COURTHOUSE
Catherine Street,
Waterford
(1849)

Designed by John B.
Keane (d. 1859) the mon-
umental form and austere
Classical detailing of the
courthouse were contrived
to convey the authority of
the judicial system.

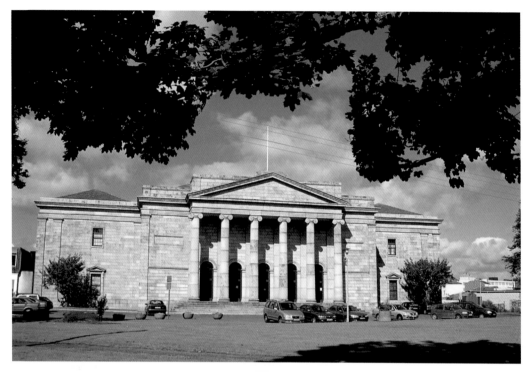

(fig. 59)
WATERFORD CITY
COURTHOUSE
Catherine Street,
Waterford

A detail of the grand
Ionic portico illustrates
the quality of the fine
carving in famously
durable Wicklow granite.

(fig. 60)
BALLYDUFF GARDA
SÍOCHÁNA STATION
Ballyduff
(1869)

Built to designs by the
Jacob Brothers on behalf
of the Board of Works,
the Scottish Baronial
stylistic treatment recalls
a similar Royal Irish
Constabulary Barracks
(1871) at Caherciveen,
County Kerry.

The erection of barracks for the Royal Irish Constabulary became the responsibility of the Board of Works following its inception. The constabulary were in the frontline of enforcing law and order, especially in response to the growing political and agrarian unrest as the century progressed. With a no-nonsense sensibility such barracks were inevitably severe in form, although many benefited from fine quality proportions and stonework. Occasionally some were designed in a more inventive manner. The Barracks (1869), Ballyduff, stands on an elevated site above the river, across the bridge from the village *(fig. 60)*. It is a fine example of the Scottish-Baronial style, complete with the associated turrets and machicolations. Designed by the Jacobs Brothers on behalf of the Board of Works, it remains in use as a barracks to this day.

The increased awareness of the benefits of education fostered the provision of schools and colleges on a scale previously unimagined and scarcely rivalled since. These were erected across the county in a variety of styles and scales, from the small picturesque village school to the large and forbiddingly institutional. The pivotal role played by Waterford in the development of religious teaching orders was inevitably reflected in much architectural effort. In 1803 the Waterford based merchant Edmund Rice (1762-1844) founded a free school for poor boys in Mount Sion School, Barrack Street. By 1823 the school was educating some 600 boys and in due course grew to become a religious teaching order, the Christian Brothers, with schools worldwide. Apart from schools provided by private patronage, the architectural department of the National Education Board undertook design responsibility. From 1856 onwards this responsibility was transferred to the Board of Works. Castlerichard School (c. 1800) is an early example of a schoolhouse in the Picturesque style *(figs. 61 - 62)*. The pointed arched windows with timber sashes and Gothic-style tracery and the arched entrance way all add to the effect. The building, on an L-shaped plan, provided accommodation for the schoolmaster, whose house retains the Lismore horizontal sash windows. It is comparable with the school in Clonea, now Scoil Cluain Fiaid Paorac Scoil Náisiúnta (1870) *(figs. 63 - 64)*. The pace of provision gathered momentum and many schools were built during the 1830s and 40s. If not quite barracks, there was a comparable sense of functionality about the buildings — education was a serious matter. The single-storey Glennawillin School (c. 1820),

(fig. 61)
CASTLERICHARD SCHOOL
Castlerichard
(c. 1800)

The small rural school comprises a single classroom block with a school master's residence to the rear. Although long disused, the school retains its original character.

(fig. 62)
CASTLERICHARD SCHOOL
Castlerichard

Gothic-style windows incorporating fine tracery detailing enhance the picturesque quality of the school. The school master's residence includes the horizontal sash windows associated with nearby Lismore.

(fig. 63)
SCOIL CLUAIN
FIAID PAORAC
SCOIL NÁISIÚNTA
Clonea
(1870)

Designed by the Board of Works, the plan of the school allowed for the segregation of pupils according to gender with one wing each linked by a shared entrance block. The division was continued in the grounds through the provision of separate play areas to the rear of the school.

(fig. 64)
SCOIL CLUAIN
FIAID PAORAC
SCOIL NÁISIÚNTA
Clonea

An inscribed stone records the name and date of construction of the school.

(fig. 65)
CARRIGNAGOWER
NATIONAL SCHOOL
Glengarra
(1843)

The plan and elevation
of the school at Glengarra
are comparable with the
D'Israeli Endowed School
(1826), Bough, in nearby
County Carlow.

(fig. 66)
BALLINVELLA
NATIONAL SCHOOL
Ballinvella
(1862)

The Board of Works stan-
dard design accommo-
dates a classroom each
for male and female
pupils, with a shared
entrance.

(fig. 67)
BALLINVELLA
NATIONAL SCHOOL
Ballinvella

A cut-stone plaque
furnishes the gable of
the school.

Sapperton, is built of exposed course rubble but benefits visually from ashlar sandstone dressings and a pedimented central bay. The five-bay Carrignagower School (1843) is somewhat more lavish *(fig. 65)*. A gabled, two-storey central bay, the schoolmaster's house, is flanked by advanced and recessed terminal bays housing the classrooms. Tall turret finials, some of which are chimneystacks, decorate the central bay. The National School (1862), Ballinvella, is typical of the standardised type of Board of Works school design produced from the mid-century onwards *(figs. 66 - 67)*. Built of rubble stone, originally rendered, it is a gabled three-bay single-storey structure with recessed side bays. The prominent datestone is one of the few decorative concessions. The imposingly large De La Salle College (1894), Waterford, stands testimony to the increasing scale of educational provision attempted at the end of the century *(fig. 68)*. Still retaining much of its original appearance, it stands proud as a three-storey over raised basement building with an imposing single-bay pedimented entrance approached by steps.

(fig. 68)
DE LA SALLE COLLEGE
Newtown Road,
Waterford
(1894)

An imposing Classically-detailed institution occupying a prominent elevated site in the south suburbs of Waterford, the De La Salle College stands as evidence of the efforts to educate the people of the city in the late nineteenth century.

Waterford City hosted the greatest variety and number of substantial public buildings, including those built for the welfare of others. Many almshouses were erected in the city. The design of the monumental Saint Otteran's Hospital (1834) has been attributed to Francis Johnson (1761-1829) and William Murray (d. 1849). It is a Classical building, austerely detailed and based on the design formula of Palladian country house architecture; a three-bay central entrance block framed by lateral wings. The main projecting entrance bay is given prominence; the doorway is flanked by paired pilasters with consoles supporting the entablature, and a fine clock tower above enhances the overall effect. The increased scale of destitution across Ireland in the nineteenth century as a whole, not just in the famine period, necessitated the provision of workhouses, which to this day retain the stigma of poverty and social injustice. However, taken on their

(fig. 69)
LISMORE UNION
WORKHOUSE
Townparks East,
Lismore
(1841)

Lismore Union Workhouse
was one of four complex-
es built in County
Waterford (including
Dungarvan, Kilmacthomas
and Waterford City) to
alleviate the economic
hardship of the peasantry,
which culminated in the
Great Famine of 1845-49.
The Governor's House,
pictured, is presently
undergoing restoration.

own merits as buildings, many were well built
with attractive architectural features and detailing. Workhouses were provided in Dungarvan
(1839-41), Kilmacthomas (1840), Waterford
City (1839-41), and Lismore. At the entrance to
the complex at Lismore the governor's house
(1841), a detached two-storey gabled stone
building of solid appearance, is built in a Tudor
Revival style *(figs. 69 - 71)*. The square-headed
windows have cut-stone sills, cut-stone surrounds, and hood mouldings over. Other decorative features include timber casement windows with diamond-leaded panels and timber
bargeboards. The freestanding workhouse proper, now in a state of disrepair, was renovated
in the 1930s when it was in use as a hospital
and nursing home.

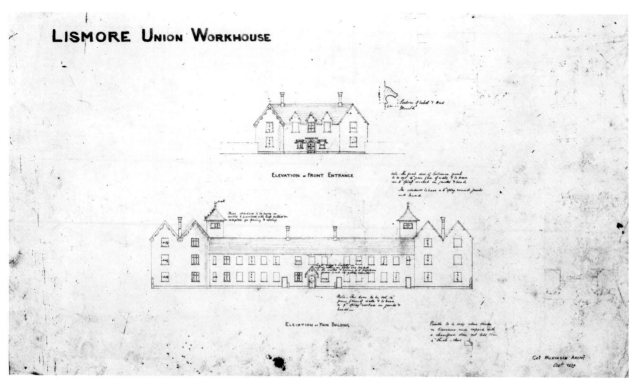

LISMORE UNION WORKHOUSE

ELEVATION of FRONT ENTRANCE

ELEVATION of MAIN BUILDING

(fig. 70)
LISMORE UNION
WORKHOUSE
Townparks East,
Lismore

A view of the plans for
Lismore Union Workhouse
complex signed and
dated by the architect
George Wilkinson
(1813/4-90) in 1839.
The workhouse illustrated
at the bottom of the
image was converted to
use as a hospital and
nursing home in the
1930s, and is now
derelict.

*Courtesy of the Irish
Architectural Archive.*

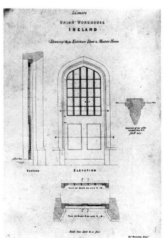

(fig. 71)
LISMORE UNION
WORKHOUSE
Townparks East,
Lismore

This doorcase, shown in
detail, was proposed for
the Governor's House at
Lismore Union Workhouse
by George Wilkinson.

*Courtesy of the Irish
Architectural Archive.*

The industrial legacy of the century tends to be overshadowed by developments elsewhere in Ireland, and in Great Britain in particular. And yet Waterford was initially well placed to develop upon an existing industrial culture, with an ample supply of water harnessed to power mills and a ready transport route to ports such as Youghal. Even if Tallow's early ironworks had not flourished the town seems to have been reasonably prosperous at the beginning of the century, with wool combing as the principal business until flourmills were constructed for the Hannans in 1822. Cotton, soon to be synonymous with Manchester, was not only manufactured at Portlaw for the home market but was also exported to the United States of America, from where the raw cotton had been imported, transferred up river, and carried by a short canal to the plant. The original mill (established 1825) was similar to its English counterparts, consisting of a tall rectangular six-storey, now five-storey, block with rows of simple windows *(figs. 72 - 74)*. The first fifteen

PORTLAW FACTORY. Co. WATERFORD. 6B. W. L.

(fig. 72)
PORTLAW
COTTON FACTORY
Factory Road (off),
Portlaw
(established 1825)

A general view of the Portlaw Cotton Factory shows the close proximity of the mill building to the Malcomson's Mayfield House. The mill pond in the foreground was filled in over the course of the twentieth century when the grounds were operating as a tannery.

Courtesy of the National Library of Ireland.

(fig. 73)
PORTLAW
COTTON FACTORY
Factory Road (off),
Portlaw

Forming the centrepiece
of the planned 'Model'
village of Portlaw, the
factory was established
by the Malcomson family
for the production of
cotton. The factory
building pictured was
built in two phases in
1825 and 1837-9.

*Courtesy of the National
Library of Ireland.*

(fig. 74)
PORTLAW
COTTON FACTORY
Factory Road (off),
Portlaw

The energy required to
operate the cotton factory
was supplied by a pair of
enormous waterwheels,
into which water from
the Clodiagh River was
channelled by a mill race.
Although the wheels are
now gone, the wheel pits
survive intact to the present day.

*Courtesy of the National
Library of Ireland.*

(fig. 75)
CLASHMORE DISTILLERY/
CLASHMORE FLOUR MILL
Clashmore
(c. 1830)

A tapered red brick
chimney survives as a
reminder of a distillery
operating in Clashmore in
the mid nineteenth centu-
ry, later converted to a
flour mill. The position of
the chimney on a rubble
stone footbridge over the
Greagagh River adds con-
siderably to its pictur-
esque value in the
townscape.

bays on the southern end were completed
before 1825, while the northern section of thir-
teen bays was built in the late 1830s. The
Malcomson project at Portlaw prospered until
the consequences of the American Civil War
(1861-5) pushed the firm into liquidation in
1876, closing the mills and prompting massive
emigration from the locality. At Clashmore
remaining high stone walls, ruined buildings,
and a tall two-storey chimney serve as a
reminder of an industrial past. The stone and
red brick chimney (c. 1830) stands on a low
two-arch stone footbridge (c. 1830) over the
River Greagagh *(fig. 75)*. A distillery operated
there in 1837, and later a flourmill in 1840.
The ruined watermill Carrigcastle Mill
(c. 1815), Ballylaneen, is now a gaunt roofless
five-storey structure *(fig. 76)*. At Knockmahon,
the ruined engine house (1824), perched on an
elevated site overlooking the sea, is a reminder
of the once thriving copper-mining industry,
owned by the Osbournes, that carried on until
closure in the 1870s *(fig. 77-78)*.

(fig. 76)
CARRIGCASTLE
(CORN) MILL
Carrigcastle
(c. 1815)

In ruins since before
1925, the mill that his-
torically supported much
of the local agricultural
economy now gives a
Romantic quality to the
landscape. A chimney,
pictured in the back-
ground, forms an impor-
tant element of the
industrial complex.

(fig. 77)
TANKARDSTOWN
COPPER MINE
Knockmahon
(Established 1824)

The remains of an engine
house and outbuildings
survive as a reminder of
the copper mine estab-
lished by the Osborne
family of Carrickbarron
and County Tipperary.
Related buildings in the
village of Knockmahon
include Osborne Terrace,
a collection of mine workers' houses, together with
a manager's house and
temperance hall.

(fig. 78)
TANKARDSTOWN
COPPER MINE
Knockmahon

The picturesque
remains of the copper
mine complex.

STRADBALLY
(c. 1800)

A small scale artefact of
the industrial heritage
of County Waterford;
the kiln was traditionally
used as a communal
means of producing
lime for agricultural
and building purposes.

The growth of trade and industry had inevitable consequences for the commercial life of towns and villages across the county. Market houses, small family run shops and public houses, often with groceries and pubs occupying the same premises, all reflect a period of expansion in trade and retail. An early market house (c. 1775), Upper Main Street, Cappoquin, may be identified by the originally open double arched arcade on the ground floor. Although it was superseded by a later market house on a different site, the original building continues to serve a commercial purpose. The proudly proclaimed family name over a private business with an attractive brightly coloured shopfront became characteristic of Irish towns. Such distinctive shopfronts have been threatened in recent decades with many swept away by post 1960s 'improvements'. Happily, several fine and varied examples from the late nineteenth century survive. These were usually made of timber or moulded render, or a combination of both materials. Their frontages incorporated motifs such as pilasters and fascia supported by ornamental consoles, recalling in a vernacular manner the fine furniture and Classical architecture of another era. Many earlier buildings were, of course, refronted or embellished in what was then considered the latest style. Cappoquin retains a fine array of original shopfronts, among them Walsh's (c. 1830), which may originally have been a farmhouse *(fig. 79)*. Later painted quoins, pilasters, fascia, and windows with panels and brackets supporting pediments add interest to the façade. Olden's (c. 1860) on Barrack Street *(figs. 80 - 81)* and Kenny's (house c. 1850; front c. 1880) on Main Street *(fig. 82)* both show the use of architec-

tural elements with pilasters, raised lettering, and moulded fascias displayed in a restrained and pleasing manner. While the building has now been converted to domestic use, another former shopfront (c. 1850) has been retained and still impresses through the use of fine pilasters and satisfying proportions *(fig. 83)*. The maintenance of the original timber framed sash windows enhances the overall effect.

MAIN STREET
Cappoquin
(c. 1890)

An archival view of Main Street illustrates a collection of commercial premises, the shopfronts of a number of which survive intact to the present day. Moore's Hotel is visible on the extreme left of the image.

Courtesy of the National Library of Ireland.

NI
NI

(fig. 79)
WALSH'S
Main Street/The
Green/Barrack Street,
Cappoquin
(c. 1830)

The building makes a
pleasing contribution to
the streetscape by jutting
out slightly from the
established line of the
street. Although it may
have originally been
built as a farmhouse,
rendered dressings
including a wrap-around
shopfront were added
in the late nineteenth
century to accommodate
commercial use.

(fig. 83)
Main Street,
Cappoquin
(c. 1850)

An early shopfront of
simple design quality has
survived the re-conver-
sion of the house to residential use. The profile
of the window openings
to the upper floors pro-
duces an attractively
tiered effect.

(fig. 80)
OLDEN
Barrack Street,
Cappoquin
(c. 1860)

The appealing purpose-
built commercial building
incorporates rendered
details and iron crested
dressings, all of which
enhance the artistic
design quality of the
composition.

(fig. 81)
OLDEN
Barrack Street,
Cappoquin

Detail of the raised
rendered lettering
applied to the
shopfront fascia.

(fig. 82)
KENNY
Main Street,
Cappoquin
(c. 1855)

This shopfront is typical
of a design influenced
by elements of the Classical
style and includes pan-
elled pilasters, decorative
consoles, and an iron
crested moulded cornice.

TWOMEY AND COMPANY
Main Street,
Cappoquin
(c. 1850)

A timber shopfront
(c. 1875) incorporating
Classical elements distinguishes a modestly
scaled building in the
streetscape.

T. UNIACKE
Main Street,
Cappoquin
(c. 1870)

Pared window openings,
colonettes, segmental-
headed surrounds, and
a rendered shopfront all
enhance the street scene
of Main Street at street
level.

MAIN STREET
Cappoquin
(c. 1840)

One of a pair of early
shopfronts in Main Street
includes robust Classical
elements such as
engaged fluted Doric
columns, and a deep
cornice.

MAIN STREET/
CASTLE STREET
Cappoquin
(c. 1840)

A symmetrical shopfront
(c. 1865) is carefully
integrated into a well
proportioned corner-
sited house.

(fig. 84)
GREEHY
Main Street,
Lismore
(c. 1790)

This shopfront is not
outwardly design con-
scious and takes the
form of remodelled
openings surmounted by
a rendered fascia board.
The form of frontage
may be considered a
true Irish traditional
model and contributes to
the urban vernacular of
the streetscape.

(fig. 85)
R. FOLEY/THE MALL BAR
Main Street/North Mall,
Lismore
(c. 1870)

This purpose-built com-
mercial building occupies
an important corner site
in the centre of Lismore.
The fine rendered detail-
ing throughout is evi-
dence of high quality
local craftsmanship.

(fig. 86)
THE ARCADE
4-5 Main Street,
Lismore
(c. 1790)

Originally built as
two separate houses, a
shopfront was inserted
in the early twentieth
century and includes
decorative timber letter-
ing to the fascia board.

(fig. 87)
THE RED HOUSE INN
Main Street/
Chapel Street,
Lismore
(1902)

A picturesque building
makes a dramatic visual
statement against the
reserved Classical treat-
ment of the Lismore
Courthouse and Lismore
Arms Hotel. Although
some features have been
lost, including profiled
slate hanging to the
gables, the building
retains many of the
essential characteristics
that contribute to the
Arts and Crafts theme.

(fig. 88)
G. KEE FABRICS
3 Barrack Street,
Waterford
(c. 1860)

The symmetrical plan of
the shopfront is in keep-
ing with the arrange-
ment of the openings to
the upper floors, produc-
ing a harmonious and
balanced composition.

(fig. 89)
J. AND K. WALSH
11 Great George's Street,
Waterford
(c. 1790)

Carefully considered fea-
tures, such as the glazed
fascia over gilded
recessed lettering, are
often absent from
replacement modern
shopfronts of little inherent design distinction.

(fig. 90)
FRANK ENGLISH
1 O'Connell Street/
Thomas Street,
Waterford
(1882)

In this instance the ren-
dered shopfront forms
part of a comprehensive
design scheme that
envelopes the entire
building with Classical
motifs such as string-
courses and cornices
present on each floor.

JOHN HEARN
87-88 Coal Quay,
Waterford
(c. 1830)

Two substantial houses
are unified at ground
floor level by a shared
timber shopfront
(c. 1880) of simple
design quality.

60-63 JOHN STREET
Waterford
(1889)

A group of four terraced
red brick houses, each of
which retains an original
timber shopfront, con-
tribute to the character
of John Street.

Greehy's (c. 1790) on Main Street, Lismore, was possibly built as two separate houses *(fig. 84)*. It was extensively renovated around 1870; simple rendered fascia and timber display windows were installed and the decorative rendered quoins added. The Mall Bar (c. 1870), also on Main Street, was a purpose-built premises occupying an important corner site *(fig. 85)*. Its handsome rendered façade with round-headed windows is enlivened by the typical features of such fronts and further embellished with a frill of wrought of iron above. The Arcade (c. 1790), 5-6 Main Street, had a timber shopfront inserted on the ground floor around 1910 *(fig. 86)*. The Red House (1902) exemplifies the Arts and Crafts style of the late nineteenth century, of which true examples are comparatively rare in Ireland *(fig. 87)*. The building has a brightly painted façade with decorative features that include a timber veran-

da balcony, oriel window and carved timber bargeboards; all essential features of the style. Its placement in the townscape, confronting the sombre courthouse on the opposite corner, as well as its scale and combination of elements, add to the overall elegance of the town. Waterford City too has retained many fine examples of the type. G. Kee Fabrics (c. 1860), Barrack Street, has panelled pilasters and a display window with a timber fascia supported on ornamented consoles *(fig. 88)*. Two upper floors, that would have been the original family's living accommodation, still have timber sash windows and original glazing. Other fine examples have been retained at 11 Great George's Street (house, c.1790; shopfront, c. 1890), the premises of J. & K. Walsh *(fig. 89)*, and 1 O'Connell Street (1882), the premises of Frank English *(fig. 90)*.

(fig. 91)
THE GRANARY/
WATERFORD MUSEUM
OF TREASURES
Merchant's Quay/
Hanover Street,
Waterford
(1872)

A solid and substantial
rubble stone warehouse
survives as a reminder of
the continued develop-
ment of an industrial
and commercial centre
about the quays in the
nineteenth century.
The warehouse has been
converted to an alterna-
tive use while retaining
important features
including the supporting
cast-iron pillars to the
interior.

Waterford City maintained its role as the main economic centre of the county. Shipbuilding became a profitable business as the century advanced and fortunes were to be made. The Penrose, Pope, and Malcomson families, among others, had their shipyards in the city. Warehousing was required for the storage of goods. The Granary (1872), Merchant's Quay, incorporates fabric from an earlier struc-ture *(fig. 91)*. The functional, but obviously secure, nature of the building is readily appar-ent. The six-storey rubble built external walls are relieved with limestone ashlar detailing, while the interior retains cast-iron columns supporting great wooden beams and the ware-house floors. It now houses the Treasures of Waterford Museum, which has managed to combine high conservation standards in main-taining the building with award winning ideas of museum practice. The increase in economic activity was mirrored by the construction of more substantial commercial buildings notably the many banks. The current Assembly House (designed 1841) on O'Connell Street was for-merly a bank built by Thomas Jackson (1807-90) *(figs. 92 - 95)*. In keeping with the styles favoured by architects of banks across the United Kingdom in these years Jackson employed the Classical idiom, in this instance using the Corinthian order. The design not only hearkened back to the Italian origins of modern banking, but exuded an air of institu-tional security and opulence, reassuring would-be customers of the bank's profitability.

(fig. 92)
ASSEMBLY HOUSE
31 O'Connell Street,
Waterford
(1841)

A handsome Classical-
style edifice built as a
branch office of the
Trustees Savings Bank
to designs prepared by
Thomas Jackson (1807-
90). The bank was origi-
nally surmounted by a
cupola, or dome, which
was dismantled in the
mid twentieth century.

(fig. 93)
COMPETITION
ENTRY FOR TRUSTEES
SAVINGS BANK
(1840)

A submission by Henry
Hill (1806/7-87) entered
into a competition for
the branch office of the
Trustees Saving Bank.
The scheme shares a
number of characteristics
in common with the
bank ultimately complet-
ed by Jackson.

*Courtesy of Myrtle Allen,
Allen Collection,
County Cork.*

(fig. 94)
COMPETITION
ENTRY FOR TRUSTEES
SAVINGS BANK

An alternative proposal
by Hill, again unsuccess-
ful, was in some respects
an inversion of his first
submission with a
recessed central block
and advanced end bays
replacing a breakfront
and recessed end bays.

*Courtesy of Myrtle Allen,
Allen Collection,
County Cork.*

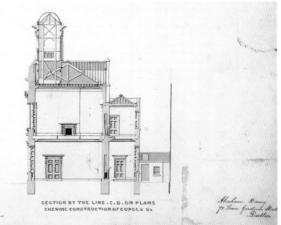

(fig. 95)
COMPETITION
ENTRY FOR TRUSTEES
SAVINGS BANK

A proposal, signed by
Abraham Denny (1820-
92), encompasses a plain
exterior topped by a
cupola. A cross section
indicates the relationship
of the banking hall with
the boardroom to the
first floor.

*Courtesy of the Irish
Architectural Archive.*

(fig. 96)
FBD INSURANCE
1 Great George's Street/
Sargent's Lane,
Waterford
(1887)

Built as a branch of the
National Bank by John
H. Brett (1835-1920) the
composition incorporates
a range of features that
appear to have been
influenced by the writ-
ings of John Ruskin
(1819-1900). The bank
stands in marked con-
trast to the refined ele-
gance of the adjacent
Morris House.

(fig. 97)
WATERFORD CITY
POST OFFICE
100 Custom House Quay/
Keizer Street,
Waterford
(1876)

The juxtaposition of
a number of building
materials, varied profiles
to the openings, and
robust detailing ensure
that James Ryan's
(fl. 1876) composition
makes a strong impact.
The building was intend-
ed to replace an earlier
custom house on site.

(fig. 98)
CLYDE HOUSE
107 The Quay/
Keizer Street,
Waterford
(c. 1890)

Constructed in red brick
with vigorous terracotta
detailing, Clyde House
makes a warm impres-
sion against the cool
grey granite of the adja-
cent post office and cus-
tom house.

The branch of the National Bank of Ireland (1887) on Great George's Street, was designed by John H. Brett (1835-1920) *(fig. 96)*. Although visually it is equally Italian, its references are inspired by the Venetian Renaissance, as mediated through the writings of the theorist John Ruskin (1819-1900), rather than the columns of Rome and Florence. Situated on a confined site, not unlike Venetian prototypes, it displays a wealth of variety and detailing, and the quality particularly admired by Ruskin of contrasting building materials: brick, marble, limestone, cast-iron; all of which acts as a foil to the Classicism of the adjoining Morris House. The Venetian Renaissance also provided inspiration for the City Post Office (1876), a much larger, quayside structure built on the site of the old customs house, which it was originally intended to replace *(fig. 97)*. It was designed by James Ryan (fl. 1876) and its superficially austere façade is relieved by the Venetian inspired motif of irregularly spaced

and varied windows, with delicate pink Corinthian colonettes on the upper storey set against the sombre grey granite. The pointed triple-bay entrance portico picks up the Venetian theme and a deep console-supported cornice caps the whole impressively scaled composition. The building, albeit imposing, was just of many architectural manifestations of the increased scope of the postal services in the period, facilitated by the growth of the railway service. Post boxes of varying shapes became commonplace in towns and villages, most incorporating the distinctive royal cipher. Adjoining the City Post Office, the red brick Clyde House (c. 1890) stands in contrast to the granite of Ryan's pile, but is equally urbane *(fig. 98)*. The influence of the short-lived Aesthetic Movement is tangibly evident in its large windows, giving light filled interiors, in the variety of its forms, and in the rich ornamental detailing of terracotta relief panels.

(fig. 100)
BOYCE COTTAGES
Tallow

Gothic-style windows
add considerably to the
picturesque charm of
the terrace and each
almshouse retains its
original character.

(fig. 101)
BOYCE COTTAGES
Tallow

A cut-stone plaque
ensures that the
benevolence of John
Boyce in the sponsorship
of the scheme is forever
apparent.

(fig. 99)
BOYCE COTTAGES
Tallow
(1830)

A group of almshouses
built for 'Aged Couples'
by John Boyce Esq., a
local landowner. The
attractive terrace is set in
enclosed grounds on the
outskirts of Tallow. A
contemporary almshouse
of similar stylistic appearance is located a short
distance away.

BALLYBRICKEN GREEN
Waterford
(c. 1890)

A view of the market or
fair day traditionally held
weekly on Ballybricken
Green, a working class
residential area devel-
oped in the nineteenth
century around the
county gaol (now gone)
and the military barracks.

*Courtesy of the National
Library of Ireland.*

In an earlier age charitable buildings had been provided by the Church, individual patrons, or landlords. In Tallow, for example, an attractive terrace of six almshouses (1830) was erected by John Boyce Esq., to house 'Aged Couples' *(figs. 99 - 101)*. In later decades, mindful of poverty in the midst of a powerful political and economic empire, boroughs and corporations showed an increased commitment to look after the less well off in society. The provision of public services, such as libraries, became the prerogative of what are now known as local authorities. The former Barker House (c. 1730) was renovated around 1880 and acted for a period as the Waterford Municipal Library. The original windows and exterior fix-tures were replaced at this time. The Corporation's first housing scheme, fulfilling 'a desire to improve the condition of the working classes', was built in Green's Lane (now Green Street) (1877). These well-built two-storey houses were joined by a further scheme, Summerhill Terrace (1890), consisting of twenty-four terraced single-storey houses. Of these, 7 Summerhill Terrace has retained many of its original features, including timber sash windows *(figs. 102 - 103)*. The milestone 'Housing of Working Class Act' (1890) led to the creation of several developments of this type of housing, especially in the area of Ballybricken Green.

(fig. 102)
7 SUMMERHILL TERRACE
Waterford
(1890)

Of a group of houses sponsored by the local authority, Number 7 is the last to retain the original bipartite windows that contribute to the architectural value of the composition.

(fig. 103)
7 SUMMERHILL TERRACE
Waterford

Many of the local authority housing schemes in the city show cast-iron plaques recording the alderman responsible for the project, together with the date of construction.

(fig. 104)
CATHOLIC CHURCH
OF THE HOLY
TRINITY WITHOUT
Ballybricken Green (off)/
Mayor's Walk (off),
Waterford
(c. 1810)

Built on the site of a
predecessor, the present
church is set in an
attractive graveyard con-
taining cut-stone markers
dating to the early eigh-
teenth century. The
handsome tower identi-
fies the church in the
low lying landscape of
Ballybricken Green.

(fig. 105)
CATHOLIC CHURCH
OF SAINT JOHN
THE BAPTIST
Crooke
(c. 1840)

Despite the ornate quali-
ty of the Gothic-style
west front, the remain-
der of the church is
comparatively austerely
treated and depends on
the correct arrangement
of openings for architec-
tural distinction.

Churches and religious houses were arguably the most accessible 'fine architecture' and reflected not only the collective aspirations of a given community, but also the personal tastes or ambitions of great patrons, individual priests, or religious leaders. They stood at the heart of existing towns and expanding urban communities, or else in open countryside, providing a focus for an otherwise scattered rural community. The nineteenth century saw an unparalleled growth in the number of churches of various denominations, their equally varied styles reflecting not only different belief systems but also the ever-changing architectural tastes of the age. Religious orders too were responsible for some of the most impressive structural design of the period.

In Waterford City, the Catholic Church of the Holy Trinity Without (c. 1810) on Ballybricken Green stood, as the name implies, outside the former city walls *(fig. 104)*. It was a pre-Emancipation church embraced by a growing community but retaining, even when altered post Second Vatican Council (1962-66), its earlier austerity along with original galleries. The imposing west tower is the most dramatic architectural concession. The plainness common to these early churches would give way, through time, to increasing lavishness applied across a range of revival styles, both Gothic and Classical. Churches in smaller rural areas inevitably kept some of the earlier simplicity, as at the church of Saint John the Baptist (c. 1840), Crooke *(fig. 105)*. In a picturesque setting, overlooking the sea, it is a medium-size single-cell church with a strong buttressed and rusticated west gable with a bellcote.

(fig. 106)
KILLROSSANTY CHURCH
Gortnalaght
(1808)

Built following the provision of a grant by the Board of First Fruits, the church adopts a standard appearance comprising a nave with vestry projection, and a slender battlemented entrance tower.

(fig. 107)
SAINT MARY'S CHURCH
Fountain
(1831)

Saint Mary's, with characteristics in common with Kilrossanty Church, confirms the influence of the Board of First Fruits in the planning of the churches that they sponsored.

While the Classical style dictated much church architecture during the previous centuries, the Gothic dominated throughout the nineteenth, although not exclusively so. In its simplest manifestation it was, as a rule, the style employed across Ireland for churches erected by the Board of First Fruits. In essence these churches consisted of rectangular planned hall spaces with the addition of a pinnacled tower often housing the entrance porch. The 'Gothic' component was often confined to straightforward lancet windows along the nave or on the tower. As Gothic Revivalism became more assured, or if the congregation was larger or more affluent, the level and quality of detailing, notably stonework, could be embellished. Later alterations or extensions tended to be in the Gothic style. Killrossanty Church (1808), Gortnalaght *(fig. 106)*, and Saint Mary's Church (1831), Fountain *(fig. 107)*, highlight the tendency. Saint Carthage's Cathedral (originally c. 1630-1675), Lismore, was subjected to

(fig. 108)
SAINT CARTHAGE'S
CATHEDRAL
North Mall,
Lismore
(1811)

The present cathedral, rebuilt by Sir Richard Morrison (1767-1844), continued a long-standing ecclesiastical presence on site. Originally founded in 675 as an enclosed monastic settlement, the building incorporates the fabric of an early seventeenth-century chancel and a late seventeenth-century nave. The tower and spire were added in 1827 by the brothers George (1793-1838) and James Pain (1779-1877).

a range of interventions and alterations over the century *(fig. 108)*. Sir Richard Morrison (1767-1844) carried out work around 1811; Owen Fahy, who worked with Morrison, had made a drawing of the neo-Gothic stone gateway as early as 1810 *(figs. 109 - 110)*. While some of the decoration on the colonettes is unfinished, similar designs are to be found on Morrison's gateway (pre-1808) at Portumna Castle, County Galway, and at Howth Castle (c. 1835), Fingal. Later work at the cathedral, still in an early phase of the Gothic Revival, was carried out around 1827 by the Pain brothers, George (1793-1838) and James (1779-1877). The interior has some fine ecclesiastical fittings executed by the firm of William Morris and Company, London. The fittings include excellent woodwork, pulpit, and screens with later stained-glass panels designed by Sir Edward Burne-Jones (1833-98) *(figs. 111 - 114)*.

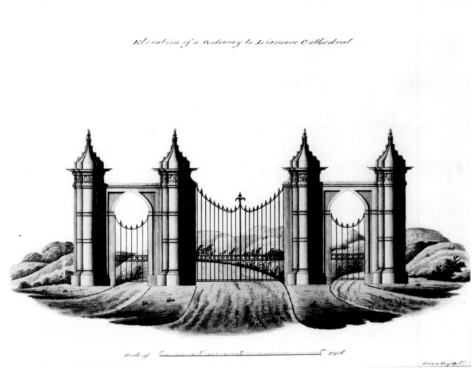

Elevation of a Gateway to Lismore Cathedral

Scale of _____ *feet*

(fig. 109)
SAINT CARTHAGE'S
CATHEDRAL
North Mall

An illustration by Owen
Fahy shows the gateway
designed by Morrison
for the grounds of Saint
Carthage's Cathedral.
Artistic licence allowed
for the inclusion of an
incongruous sweeping
landscape in the back-
ground that fails to
include the cathedral
proper.

*Courtesy of the Irish
Architectural Archive.*

(fig. 110)
SAINT CARTHAGE'S
CATHEDRAL
North Mall,
Lismore

Completed in 1831,
the gateway at Lismore
recalls similar schemes
prepared by Morrison
for the entrances to
Portumna Castle (pre-
1808), County
Waterford, and Howth
Castle (c. 1835), Fingal.
On closer inspection it is
apparent that some of
the finer detail to the
rear elevation was not
fully executed.

(fig. 111)
SAINT CARTHAGE'S
CATHEDRAL
North Mall,
Lismore

A drawing by Henry
Hill illustrates the south
transept as it appeared
in 1831.

*Courtesy of the Cork
Public Museum.*

(fig. 112)
SAINT CARTHAGE'S
CATHEDRAL
North Mall,
Lismore

A view of one of the
delicate stained glass
panels executed (1896)
by Sir Edward Burne-
Jones (1833-98), in this
instance depicting
allegorical characters
of Justice and Humility.
The figures are captured
in an elegant pre-
Raphaelite setting that is
an attribute of the
artist's work.

(fig. 113)
SAINT CARTHAGE'S
CATHEDRAL
North Mall,
Lismore

A view of the interior of
the cathedral shows the
high quality artistry and
craftsmanship of the fine
timber joinery and deli-
cate plasterwork.

(fig. 114)
SAINT CARTHAGE'S
CATHEDRAL
North Mall,
Lismore

The groin-vaulted ceiling
incorporates robust
plasterwork accents.

(fig. 115)
SAINT JOHN'S CHURCH
Ballycahane
(1849)

Saint John's was built to
designs submitted by
William Tinsley (1804-85)
to replace the earlier
Clonagam Church; the
foundation stone was
laid by George Wilson
(1743-1850). The juxta-
position of a variety of
building materials and
profiled details produces
a busy polychromatic
and textured composi-
tion far removed from
the simplicity of the
church it succeeded.

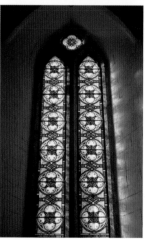

(fig. 116)
SAINT JOHN'S CHURCH
Ballycahane

Delicate stained glass
panels permit colour
saturated light to enter
the church, producing a
jewel-like visual effect.

Occasionally estates had their own 'estate church'. Saint John's Church (1849), Guilcagh *(figs. 115 - 116)*, was designed by William Tinsley (1804-1885) for Lady W. Louisa Stuart on the Curraghmore Demesne; the new building replaced the old Clonagam Church (1741) *(fig. 117)*. The cornerstone was laid May 1849 and the building was consecrated September 1852. It is built in the style of the Gothic Revival with a three-bay nave, deep chancel, gabled porch, bellcote, and buttresses. The interior is simple with a hammer beam truss roof and cantilevered stone pulpit. The establishment of a Cistercian community near Cappoquin in the early 1830s resulted in one of the best-recognised religious houses in Ireland which, in keeping with historical precedent, embarked on a prolonged building campaign. An abbey church (1920s) was built to rise above the surrounding noviciate (c. 1850) and support farm buildings (c. 1870). As the community grew in prestige it was, by the middle of the century, in a position to embark on further building campaigns. This resulted in an attractive range of a boarding houses (c. 1850) tiered in a stepped arrangement along the slope of hill with the complex terminating in a small Catholic chapel (c. 1850) in the Gothic Revival style *(fig. 118)*.

(fig. 117)
CLONAGAM CHURCH
Curraghmore
(1741)

A plain Gothic-style
single-cell church of a
type that was ultimately
superseded by the
Tinsley model now hous-
es a collection of fine
cut-stone mausoleums.

(fig. 118)
MOUNT MELLERAY
MONASTERY
Mountmelleray
(c. 1850)

A terrace of six boarding
houses is attractively
grouped in a stepped
arrangement that follows
the topography of a
sloping site. The varied
building materials give
an individual identity to
each house and the
terrace is terminated at
one end by an elaborate
Gothic Revival chapel.

(fig. 119)
PRESENTATION
CONVENT
Slievekeale Road,
Waterford
(1848-56)

Built to the designs
of Augustus Welby
Northmore Pugin (1812-
52), the convent is
arranged on a quadrangle
about a courtyard and
incorporates a chapel in
the north range.

(fig. 120)
PRESENTATION
CONVENT
Slievekeale Road,
Waterford

The chapel interior
remains substantially
intact and incorporates
a lavish decorative
scheme and fine timber
joinery. The survival of
the rood screen is
particularly noteworthy.

SAINT JOHN'S MANOR
Church Road,
Waterford
(c. 1840)

This medium sized house in the Gothic style was built for the Wyse family to a design attributable to Augustus Welby Northmore Pugin (1812-52). Polychromatic brick work with cut-stone detailing produces an aesthetically pleasing visual effect.

Courtesy of the National Library of Ireland.

(fig. 121)
CATHOLIC CHURCH
OF SAINT HELENA
OF THE CROSS
Glennanore
(c. 1865)

A medium sized church of solid form and austere detailing designed by James Joseph McCarthy (1817-82), together with the contemporary adjacent school, forms the nucleus of a small scale rural settlement.

The Gothicism apparent in churches and ecclesiastical buildings in general was subject to the influence of Augustus Welby Northmore Pugin (1812-52). Through his influential writings and executed work, Pugin produced a greater awareness of archaeological exactitude in interpreting the Gothic past, together with an attention to fine materials and the decorative possibilities of contrasts in texture and colour. His influence was considerable both across Waterford and throughout Ireland, especially the south east, as well as internationally. He was responsible for Presentation Convent (1848-56), Waterford City, an impressive convent building with inventive massing and stone detailing *(figs. 119 - 120)*. The convent clearly illustrates a key concept of Pugin's architectural philosophy: that the components of a building should be readily understandable through their exterior form. Pugin's most prolific and accomplished follower in Ireland was James Joseph McCarthy (1817-82). McCarthy is understood to be at his best in small rural churches, and his design for Nier Catholic Church (c. 1865), Labartt's Bridge, would seem to prove the point *(fig. 121)*. It is a small single cell church in the Gothic Revival manner, built of polychrome sandstone with a deep sanctuary and west tower. The lucid exterior massing is complemented by a plain interior, lit by lancet windows, with an open truss timber roof. The church forms an attractive group with an adjacent school (c. 1865) of similar appearance. Holy Cross Church (1856-71), Tramore, and the parish churches in (1858-9) and Clonea (1860), were also designed by McCarthy.

(fig. 122)
SAINT SAVIOUR'S
DOMINICAN
(CATHOLIC) CHURCH
Bridge Street/
O'Connell Street,
Waterford
(1872-80)

A monumental composition in the Italianate style, the church was built to the designs of George Goldie (1798-1868) and occupies a prominent corner site in the city. Scheduled for demolition in the late twentieth century, the church was subsequently restored and continues to serve the local community.

(fig. 123)
SAINT SAVIOUR'S
DOMINICAN
(CATHOLIC) CHURCH
Bridge Street/
O'Connell Street,
Waterford

Fine carved detailing furnishes the frontispiece of the church and enhances the ornamental quality of the composition.

Side by side with the interest in Gothic architecture and decoration, Classicism and its variants continued to be a popular design idiom. Indeed, within certain strands of Catholicism the Classical style was considered more Christian: its columns and décor reminiscent of the Rome of Antiquity, and thereby the earlier history of the Church. In some guises the use of Classical forms had political overtones equating with ultramontanisim (advocating supreme papal authority) and the influence of Cardinal Paul Cullen (1803-78), especially in the period following the Vatican Council (1870). In Waterford City, the large Domincan Church of Saint Saviour (1872-80) on Bridge Street, designed by George Goldie (1798-1868), embraced this Italianate Renaissance Revival style *(figs. 122 - 123)*. Its five-bay entrance façade combines a pedimented frontispiece framed by giant Corinthian pilasters, incorporating statue filled niches and a sculptural relief over the main entrance. The distinctive window, semi-circular with two vertical mullions, inserted in the pediment is known as a Diocletian or thermal window and enhances the intended Roman effect. The asymmetrically placed dome-capped bell tower is a distinctive and attractive feature on the Waterford skyline. The Italianate feel is carried through into the interior where arcades of polished granite Corinthian columns separate the nave and aisles, the whole enhanced with decorative plasterwork, mosaics, and a reredos of imported Italian marble. The façade (1893-7) added to Roberts's Cathedral of the Holy Trinity was no less Italian, with the Classical elements recalling any number of such façades in late sixteenth- or early seventeenth-century Rome *(figs. 124 - 125)*. It acts as a centrepiece to

(fig. 124)
CATHOLIC CATHEDRAL
OF THE HOLY TRINITY
Barronstrand Street,
Waterford
(1893-7)

Previously hemmed in by
undistinguished buildings
and concealed from
view, John Robert's
cathedral was opened on
to Barronstrand Street in
the late nineteenth cen-
tury. An elegant pedi-
mented Ionic frontispiece
incorporating a break-
front was finally installed
over one hundred years
after the construction of
the cathedral com-
menced.

(fig. 125)
CATHOLIC CATHEDRAL
OF THE HOLY TRINITY
Barronstrand Street,
Waterford

An archival view (c.
1890) of Barronstrand
Street depicts cast-iron
gates and railings following the line of the buildings cleared to reveal the
cathedral. The gates
were removed in the late
twentieth century to fur-
ther open out the street
frontage of the site.

*Courtesy of the National
Library of Ireland.*

(fig. 126)
SAINT CATHERINE'S HALL
Catherine Street/
Waterside,
Waterford
(1860)

The paired towers recalling an Italianate palazzo were characteristic of the work of Abraham Denny (1820-92). The construction in red brick with polychromatic dressings contrasts with the cool austerity of the adjacent courthouse.

Courtesy of the Irish Architectural Archive.

(fig. 127)
SAINT CATHERINE'S HALL
Catherine Street/
Waterside,
Waterford

A cut-stone plaque proudly records the name and date of establishment of the institution.

(fig. 128)
SAINT CATHERINE'S HALL
Catherine Street/
Waterside,
Waterford

Cast-iron street name signs are gradually being replaced with modern versions of lesser aesthetic qualities.

Barronstrand Street and complements the Classical idiom of the earlier interior. It is articulated with tall Ionic pilasters while paired pilasters frame the pedimented three-bay main entrance. The decorated pediment rises through a rooftop balustrade on which statues pick up the vertical thrust of the elements below, once again evoking Italian prototypes and reminding the viewer of the Roman nature of the church. The interior was altered at various dates throughout the century. The carved timber galleries and much of the stained glass work by Meyer of Munich formed part of these alterations. The Protestant hall (Saint Catherine's Hall) and Sunday school (1860) on Catherine Street, Waterford, also used the Classical style *(figs. 126 - 128)*. A substantial complex of red brick with granite decorative stonework it incorporates a variety of window types, all enriched with motifs appropriate to the Renaissance Revival style. Cast-iron railings with openwork piers and cast-iron double gates enhance the appearance of the building, which was designed by Abraham Denny (1820-92), Dublin architect and sometime Waterford Corporation Alderman.

Large private houses continued to be built, and many others refurbished or enlarged, in response to changing fashions and tastes. In spite of the variety of architectural styles punctuating the century, Classicism and variants thereof dominated most large-scale domestic architecture. Substantial farmhouses and parochial houses, even where lacking the decorative detailing, favoured the qualities of scale and balance synonymous with Classical styles. Ballynatray House, the third house on the site, was refurbished (1795-7) in such a manner: the façade rendered and embellished with an elegant Ionic porch *(fig. 129)*. The house was

(fig. 129)
BALLYNATRAY HOUSE
Ballynatray Demesne
(1795-7)

Built by Grice Smyth, the
present house, the third
on the site, incorporates
the fabric of an earlier
structure (c. 1700).
Fine applied detailing
(1806) by Alexander
Deane (c. 1760-1806)
was repaired as part of a
comprehensive restora-
tion programme in 1998.

(fig. 130)
SION HILL HOUSE
Dock Road,
Waterford
(c. 1820)

Built by the Pope family
on an elevated site over-
looking their shipyards
on North Wharf, the
house includes Regency
style features such as
Classical proportions and
overhanging eaves.

(fig. 131)
SION HILL HOUSE
Dock Road,
Waterford

Freestanding pavilions
flank the entrance
front of Sion Hill House,
enhancing the formal
quality of the
composition.

comprehensively restored in 1998. A new bridge across the Suir, linking Waterford City to Ferrybank, encouraged the merchant classes to erect a range of substantial villas that not only benefited from elevated sites but also afforded their owners a picturesque vista of their city across the river. Sion Hill House (c. 1820), built for a member of the wealthy Pope family, overlooked their riverside shipyards. This substantial house, enhanced by a portico and flanking pavilions, employed the proportions of the phase of Classicism commonly known as Regency *(figs. 130 - 131)*. The stables were located near the present docks and were later used to house railway workers.

By the 1840s the ongoing taste for Classical houses encouraged a reappraisal, as with church architecture, of sixteenth-century Italian Renaissance decorative modes. Stucco decoration was frequently applied to earlier buildings by employing raised decorative detailing, architraves and the like, in the so-called Italianate manner. The alterations to the Morris House, Waterford City, were in this idiom. Samuel Ussher Roberts (1827-1900), a grandson of John Roberts, is credited with the late century encasing of the main block of Curraghmore House (originally c. 1755) *(fig. 132)*. Over the entrance, the dramatic rooftop sculpture of the stag of Saint Hubert, the family crest, carved by Sir Richard Boehm (1834-90), enhances the sense of drama of an otherwise plain façade. On occasion the embellishment amounted to a comprehensive re-casing of an earlier property, completely altering its appearance. Such was the case at Mayfield

(fig. 132)
CURRAGHMORE HOUSE
Curraghmore
(c. 1875)

Samuel Ussher Roberts (1813-92), a relative of John Roberts, enveloped the main block of Curraghmore in a cohesive stylistic skin that united the disparate components of two centuries of building programmes.

MAYFIELD HOUSE, PORTLAW, 66. W.L.

(fig. 134)
MAYFIELD HOUSE
Portlaw

Following the liquidation of the Malcomson enterprise the house became the administration centre of the tannery that succeeded the cotton factory. The house has fallen into ruin since the closure of the tannery in the 1980s.

(fig. 135)
MAYFIELD HOUSE
Portlaw

A detail of the fine carved stone detailing that embellishes the entrance tower of Mayfield House.

(fig. 133)
MAYFIELD HOUSE
Portlaw
(c. 1840)

The early (c. 1740) house was comprehensively reconstructed by William Tinsley (1804-85) for the Malcomson family to include signature motifs such as bow-ended wings. A tower added by John Skipton Mulvany (1813-71) in 1857 forms a focal point of the composition, although the awkward correspondence of levels at the junction highlights the later provenance.

Courtesy of the National Library of Ireland.

House (c. 1840), erected for the Malcomsons on a site adjoining, but screened from, their industrial plant at Portlaw *(figs. 133 - 135)*. The design is attributed to William Tinsley. The tower was added at a later date (1857) by J.S. Mulvany and, while sitting a little uncomfortably with the rest of the house, enhances its Italianate quality. In rising above the treetops it recalls the feel of an Italian belvedere but also echoes similar elements at Trentham Hall, Staffordshire (1834-40), by Sir Charles Barry (1795-1860). The design is also reminiscent of

(fig. 136)
MAYFIELD HOUSE
Factory Road,
Portlaw

Taken at the height
of the success of the
cotton factory, an
archival image (c. 1890)
shows the gate lodge
and gateway leading to
Mayfield House.

*Courtesy of the Irish
Architectural Archive.*

(fig. 138)
MAYFIELD HOUSE
Factory Road,
Portlaw

Ornate cast-iron
railings were fashioned
at the Richard Turner
Hammersmith Ironworks,
Ballsbridge, County
Dublin.

(fig. 137)
MAYFIELD HOUSE
Factory Road,
Portlaw
(1840)

Two sets of concave
cast-iron double gates,
one leading to Mayfield
House and the other to
the factory complex,
were opened by a chain

mechanism operated by
turning the wheel pic-
tured. Despite the dilapidated condition of the
gates, the mechanism
survives intact and is still
in working order.

the Italianate villa of Osborne House (1846) on
the Isle of Wight, catering for the tastes of
Prince Albert (1819-61), the prince consort of
Queen Victoria (1819-1901). Although much of
the original detail has been removed, Mayfield
House remains an imposing structure. Its
attractive gate lodge (c. 1840) stands behind a
handsome screen of decorative cast-iron gates
and piers *(figs. 136 - 138)*. The gates, designed
by Richard Turner (1798-1881), were operated
by an ingenious chain mechanism that remains
intact to this day. Tinsley is also attributed
with the design of Woodlock (now Saint
Joseph's Convent) (1864), Portlaw, another
Malcomson home.

THE LODGE, WOODLOCK, PORTLAW, 70. W. L.

WOODLOCK (HOUSE)
(SAINT JOSEPH'S
CONVENT)
Carrick Road,
Portlaw
(1864)

A small-scale gate lodge
was designed by William
Tinsley (1804-85) in an
Italianate style comple-
mentary to the appear-
ance of Woodlock
(House). The gate lodge
was lost following the
conversion of the house
to use as a convent.

*Courtesy of the National
Library of Ireland.*

Whitfield Court (built 1841-3), Kilmeaden, standing on a dramatic site overlooking a steep-sided valley, also employed this Italianate style *(fig. 139)*. The house is attributed to Daniel Robertson (fl. 1812-49) who had a wide practice in the south east of the country. The asymmetrical quality of the façade derives from the twin towers added at a later date by Abraham Denny. These recall the towers used by Denny on Saint Catherine's Hall.

(fig. 139)
WHITFIELD COURT
Dooneen
(1841-3)

Designed by Daniel
Robertson (fl. 1812-49)
the composition recalls
the architect's work in
the Classical style in
neighbouring County
Wexford, notably
Ballinkeele House,
Ballymurn. Later towers
(c. 1850), added by
Abraham Denny (1820-
92), augment the
Italianate quality of
the design.

(fig. 140)
LISMORE CASTLE
Lismore
(1812 and 1849)

A rambling pile in the Gothic Revival style, Lismore Castle is based on a quadrangle centred about a courtyard. Reconstructed over two periods in the nineteenth century, the castle has its origins in a tower house granted to Sir Walter Raleigh (1552-1618) in the sixteenth century.

(fig. 141)
LISMORE CASTLE
Lismore

A detail of the Devonshire coat-of-arms in the grounds of Lismore Castle.

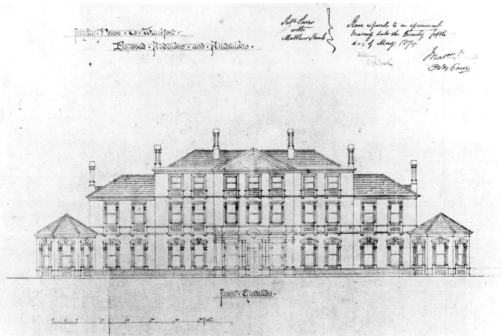

FAITHLEGG HOUSE
Faithlegg
(1783)

Originally built in the late eighteenth century for Cornelius Bolton, these drawings, signed and dated by Walter Doolin (1850-1902) in 1874, contain proposals for an expansion programme by the Power family that included the embellishment of the Classical frontages. The renovation project was ultimately carried out by Samuel Ussher Roberts (1813-92).

Courtesy of the Irish Architectural Archive.

Lismore Castle (originally 1612) is among the best-known private residences in the county and has long been the Irish seat of the Dukes of Devonshire. Its dramatic site above the River Blackwater is best appreciated when approaching from Cappoquin and, often reproduced, was fully in keeping with the picturesque tastes of the early decades of the century *(figs. 140 - 141)*. Complementing the commitment to their estates made in Lismore, Dungarvan, and elsewhere, the castle was restored and largely rebuilt by the architect William Atkinson (1773-1839) for the 6th Duke in a programme of works beginning in 1812. Building work continued at Lismore Castle throughout the first half of the century with the addition of battlemented ranges that enhanced the sense of medievalism. Sir Joseph Paxton (1803-65), associated with the Devonshire estate at Chatsworth and most famously the Crystal Palace (1851) for the Great Exhibition, had worked on a number of ranges in this medieval manner. The same effect was carried through much of the interior scheme, most spectacularly in the great banqueting hall where the much sought after and emulated decorator, John Gregory Crace (1808-89) excelled himself in evoking a fanciful medieval interior with extensive stained glass windows and stencilling. The ornate chimneypiece, the focus of this the largest room in the castle, was designed by Pugin, the whole ensemble recalling Pugin's early stage design career.

SALTERBRIDGE HOUSE
Salterbridge
(1849)

A substantial Classical-style mansion built for the Chearnly family possibly incorporates the fabric of an earlier mid eighteenth-century house, and forms the centrepiece of an extensive planned estate.

(fig. 142)
BALLYSAGGARTMORE
HOUSE
Ballysaggartmore
(c. 1845)

A certain excess is evident in the design and detailing of the gateway at Ballsaggartmore. Although originally part of a comprehensive redevelopment of the estate, ultimately funds were drained and the main house (now demolished) failed to be remodelled in a comparably ornate manner.

BALLYSAGGSARTMORE
HOUSE
Ballysaggartmore
(c. 1845)

An ornamental bridge in a robust Gothic style furnishes the grounds of Ballysaggartmore and is accessed by a gateway at either end. Almost identical in appearance on initial viewing, each gate incorporates subtle structural variations.

(fig. 143)
FORTWILLIAM HOUSE
Fortwilliam
(1836)

Built for J.B. Gumbleton, the house was comprehensively restored in the late twentieth century following a fire, with most of the original features carefully replicated. Fortwilliam House now makes a pleasing impression overlooking the River Blackwater, with gables and pinnacles enlivening the skyline.

The taste for Gothic Revival became more evident as the century progressed. Atkinson was at the heart of the developing taste for past styles, having embellished the fanciful home of Sir Walter Scott, Abbotsford in Roxburghshire, Scotland, in the 1820s. This fondness for the Gothic past was initially expressed in ornamental structures, gate lodges, hunting lodges and the like. Such buildings often assumed, perhaps unintentionally, the effect of Romantic stage scenery in the countryside, adding a sense of occasion as a visitor approached a great house. Such is the case of the gateway and lodges (c. 1820) at Ballysaggartmore, Lismore. Identical crenellated lodges with angle turrets diagonally flank the arched and pinnacled entranceway *(fig. 142)*. Fortwilliam (1836), Lismore *(fig. 143)*, was probably designed by the English architects James (1779-1877) and George Richard (1793-1838) Pain, the latter a pupil of John Nash (1752-1835). The building displays the same picturesque concept of Gothic, as do a number of castellated bridges.

The Gothic Revival style was also favoured for memorials and monuments such as the relatively ornate freestanding clock tower (1861-3) on the junction of Meagher' Quay and Coal Quay, Waterford *(fig. 144)*. One of the best-known landmarks in the city, the quality stonework of the clock tower is a testament to the long tradition of fine masonry in the county. It was originally intended as a public water supply, including drinking bowls for dogs! Although, not quite in the Gothic Revival manner, the Holroyd-Smyth Mausoleum (1876) *(figs. 145 - 146)* in Templemichael Churchyard (1823) suggested the taste for medievalism and incorporates a prominent heraldic sculpture. The cult of the dead is also celebrated, in this instance for a dog, in the monument (1873) near Dungarvan to the famous greyhound Master McGrath *(figs. 147 - 148)*.

(fig. 144)
THE CLOCK TOWER
Meagher's Quay/
Coal Quay,
Waterford
(1861-3)

This elaborate High Victorian public monument fulfilled two civic functions, one of which was as a public water supply. The tower resembles a displaced church spire in form, sitting prominently on Waterford's quayside.

(fig. 145)
HOLROYD-SMYTH
MAUSOLEUM
Templemichael Church,
Templemichael
(1876)

The medieval style of
this small scale mau-
soleum is identified by
the solid masonry walls
having little apparent
relief in the form of
openings or decorative
motifs.

(fig. 146)
HOLROYD-SMYTH
MAUSOLEUM
Templemichael Church,
Templemichael

A view of the cut-stone
Holroyd-Smyth coat-of-
arms set into the gable
of the mausoleum.

(fig. 147)
MASTER McGRATH
MONUMENT
Ballymacmague
(1873)

The erection of an ele-
gant Classical-style monument attests to the high
esteem in which Master
McGrath, a champion
greyhound, was held by
his keeper, James Galwey.
Originally located at
Colligan Lodge, the
monument was moved
to its present prominent
setting in 1933.

(fig. 148)
MASTER McGRATH
MONUMENT
Ballymacmague

A detail of the panel
framing a bas-relief
portrait of Master
McGrath.

(fig. 149)
LE POER TOWER
Tower Hill,
Clonagam
(1783)

Inspired by the medieval Irish round tower this monument, erected by the Earl of Tyrone, alludes to the contemporary taste for indigenous architectural styles. The tower makes a pleasing local landmark.

The picturesque Gothic encouraged openness to a diversity of styles, most often manifest in interior decorations schemes, but occasionally on a larger scale too. Although dating from the late eighteenth century the Le Poer Tower (1783), a memorial standing on the crest of a hill overlooking the demesne at Curraghmore, was built in the form of an Irish round tower, an early instance of taste for the 'exotic' *(fig. 149)*. Gardenmorris House (c. 1820), Kill, was rebuilt in the middle of the century in a manner recalling a French château. The Hindu-Gothic gateway (1849) at the Dromana estate, with minarets and diminutive dome, is a charming example of eclectic taste *(figs. 150 - 151)*. It replaced a temporary structure erected in the same style (1826) to celebrate the return of Henry Villiers-Stuart and his new wife from their wedding trip, and recalls on a greatly reduced scale and in a country setting, something of the effect of the Prince Regent's Brighton Pavilion (1802-21). It was given solid form in designs, dated 1849, by Martin Day (fl. 1820-40) who had designed Dromana House in 1827. The gateway was restored by the Irish Georgian Society (1967-8). Occasionally, conflicting tastes stood

(fig. 150)
DROMANA HOUSE
Mountrivers/Affane
(1849)

Designed by Martin Day
(fl. 1820-40), the present
gateway replaced a tem-
porary version erected in
celebration of the mar-
riage of Henry Villiers-
Stuart in 1826. The dis-
tinctive Hindu-Gothic
details are believed to
have been influenced by
John Nash's (1752-1835)
Royal Pavilion, Brighton
(1815-22). An archival
image illustrates the
original timber bridge
(replaced, 1970s) leading
to the gateway.

*Courtesy of the Irish
Architectural Archive.*

(fig. 151)
DROMANA HOUSE
Mountrivers/Affane

Restored by the
Georgian Society
(1967-8), and again
by Waterford County
Council (1990), the gate-
way makes a dramatic
impression and remains
a highly individual fea-
ture of the architectural
heritage of the county.

SAINT JAMES CHURCH
Church Lane,
Stradbally
(1786)

A plain, small scale
church of rustic quality
forms a focal point in the
village of Stradbally.

SAINT JAMES CHURCH
Church Lane,
Stradbally

The plain quality of the
exterior is mirrored in the
simple decorative scheme
to the nave and chancel.

(fig. 152)
STRADBALLY RECTORY
The Square,
Stradbally
(c. 1820 and c. 1870)

A house of two distinct
periods of construction,
the rectory juxtaposes a
complex Tudor-style
block with a Georgian-
style earlier portion, rele-
gated to use as a return.

(fig. 153)
BUSHFIELD (HOUSE)
Gallows Hill/West Street/
Ballyanchor Street,
Lismore
(1899)

A timber clad, timber
frame construction and
corrugated-iron roof identify Bushfield (House) as a
precursor to the self-build
kit house.

side by side, as at the Old Rectory (c. 1820),
Stradbally where a large Georgian-style house
incorporated mid century (c. 1870) additions in
a Tudor Revival style *(fig. 152)*.

Variations on the Gothic Revival theme
allowed for an embrace of other early styles
including the Tudor Revival, which, as the
name implies, evoked the 'feel' of early sixteenth-century English architecture, accurately
or otherwise. Gurteen le Poer (1866),
Kilsheelan, was designed in this style by the
clearly versatile Samuel Ussher Roberts
(fig. 154). The house combines a main block,
service wing, and prominent battlemented tower, all arranged in a picturesque composition.
The ensemble appears like a lesser Lismore
Castle, but with detailing such as decorative
gables and mullioned windows on the garden
façade to affirm its Tudor aspirations. The
Island (1895), now Waterford Castle Hotel, was
built for Gerald Purcell-Fitzgerald on an island
downstream from Waterford City, and illustrates the sustained interest in medievalism
that continued throughout the century
(fig. 156). In spite of the technological
advances characterising the century, with steel
and concrete already in use across the world,
the castle, built on the cusp of the new century, exuded an air of the distant past. Enclosing

GURTEEN LE POER
Gurteen Lower
(1866)

Designed by Samuel
Ussher Roberts (1813-92)
on behalf of the First
Count de la Poer, the
house is reminiscent of
the work of Daniel
Robertson (fl. 1812-49)
in the Tudor Revival style,
particularly Carrigglas
Manor, Longford
(1837-40).

a medieval tower with stepped battlements on
its exterior, it has a range of rooms decorated
in a manner befitting the original era of its
core structure. The principal rooms have ceiling plasterwork in the Tudor manner with
complementing panelled walls. Although providing a rare example of a surviving prefabri-
cated house from the period Bushfield (1899),
Gallow's Hill, Lismore, was nonetheless built in
a style evoking the Tudor Revival. Elements
such as box-bay windows, entrance porch, and
tall yellow brick chimneys sit side by side with
a pitched roof of corrugated iron *(fig. 153)*.

Service buildings to great houses were generally architecturally distinguished. Indeed, on
occasion, it could be argued that ranges such
as stables and gate lodges could display more
architectural inventiveness and playfulness
than the main residence. The service wings at
Curraghmore House are particularly noteworthy, and the great bulk of Lismore Castle belies
the fact that much of the castle was taken up
with administrative ranges. At other estates and
large farms the service elements were simpler
but no less pleasing aesthetically. While pre-
dating the main house, the stables (1839) at
Gurteen le Poer were incorporated in the later
project and now form the north range of the
courtyard *(fig. 155)*.

GURTEEN LE POER
Gurteen Lower
(1839)

The use of Classical
elements in the design
of the stable complex is
in contrast to the Tudor
Revival quality of the
main house; this indicates
different periods of con-
struction as well as the
lack of a cohesive stylistic
identity for the long term
development of the
estate.

WATERFORD CASTLE
HOTEL (ISLAND CASTLE)
Little Island
(1895)

Designed by Romayne
Walker (n. d.) and super-
vised by Albert Murray
(1849-1924), the castle
incorporates at least two
earlier phases of building,
including a medieval cas-
tle. The unrefined rubble
stone construction pro-
duces an attractively textured visual effect offset
by fine cut-stone details.

Smaller scaled houses, taken together with their service buildings, contribute greatly to the character of the county. Annestown House (c. 1820), located in an attractive setting overlooking the sea, is made up of two separate early nineteenth-century buildings joined together. The detached outbuildings (c. 1850s) range about a courtyard to the south of the main house. In the nearby village of Dunhill, a thatched house (c. 1820) has a two-storey addition to the more traditional single-storey range *(fig. 157)*. A small outbuilding and enclosing wall completes this unusual composition. Another surviving thatched house, Cove Cottage (c. 1810), Stradbally, is built more in the manner of the cottage orné than a traditional cottage; its distinctive windows reveal the influence of James Wyatt *(fig. 158)*. The nearby Woodstown House (1823) exemplifies the type of elegant Regency-style houses designed by George Richard Pain *(figs. 159 - 160)*. Some of the smaller farm complexes in the county, built in the vernacular rather than formal style, possess great character. The farm at Gortanadiha Upper (c. 1850) consists of a thatched farmhouse overlooking a substantial farmyard with single-storey and two-storey farm buildings arranged at right angles to the house *(fig. 161)*. A series of steps leads up to the farmhouse.

(fig. 157)
DUNHILL
(c. 1820)

An appealing thatched cottage forms the centrepiece of a vernacular farm holding, occupying an important corner site in the centre of Dunhill.

(fig. 158)
COVE COTTAGE
Nunnery Lane,
Stradbally
(c. 1810)

The picturesque composition of the cottage combines features of the vernacular idiom with elements of formal Classicism, including elegant tripartite windows derived from the work of James Wyatt (1747-1813).

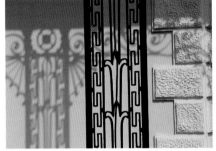

(fig. 159)
WOODSTOWN HOUSE
Woodstown Lower
(1823)

The graceful Regency-
style house was built for
Robert Shapland Carew
(d. 1829), 1st Lord
Carew, by George
Richard Pain (1793-
1838). Balanced propor-
tions and fine rendered
detailing enhance the
architectural value of
the composition.

(fig. 160)
WOODSTOWN HOUSE
Woodstown Lower

A delicate iron veranda
contributes to the
elegant quality of
Woodstown House.

(fig. 161)
GORTNADIHA UPPER
(c. 1850)

An assortment of mod-
estly scaled farm build-
ings, each of vernacular
significance, is arranged
about a courtyard in a
manner characteristic of
the south east of Ireland.

(fig. 162)
SALLYHENE COTTAGES
Knocknacrohy
(c. 1860)

A collection of eight estate workers' houses incorporates decorative elements, such as diamond leaded windows and profiled timber joinery, which enhance the architectural design quality of the group.

(fig. 163)
SALLYHENE COTTAGES
Knocknacrohy

Iron door furnishings provide subtle decorative incident to the houses.

Farm buildings, in many respects housing the lifeblood of the estate, were accompanied on larger estates by an array of buildings often of architectural interest. These include churches as at Curraghmore, gate lodges, estate cottages, follies, and boathouses. Sallyhene Cottages (c. 1860) were erected on the estate at Curraghmore as four pairs of small semi-detached residences *(figs. 162 - 163)*. While functional they contributed a picturesque quality through the incorporation of casement windows and timbered porches. The demesne at Strancally Castle (1826-1860) houses a charming example of an ornamental thatched cottage (c. 1850) with a veranda and slender iron columns supporting deep eaves and a thatched roof. Dating from the middle of the century it recalls the once widespread taste for the picturesque, of which the artfully designed cottage orné formed part. Many designs for such cottages were published throughout the century. Other estate cottages, such as those at Sapperton (c. 1840), lacked the typical array of decorative features, but in their plainness were no less pleasing *(fig. 164)*.

STRANCALLY CASTLE
Strancally Demesne
(c. 1855)

Open work piers and cast-iron gates and railings combine to produce a feature of artistic design distinction.

(fig. 164)
SAPPERTON HOUSE
Sapperton South
(c. 1840)

The primary emphasis is placed on the provision of adequate accommodation for estate workers and the pair of cottages has minimal architectural pretension.

STONEHOUSE
(c. 1800)

Stout buttresses supporting the walls are a feature common to vernacular buildings, and particularly in cottages of mud wall construction.

KILRUSH COTTAGE
Kilrush
(c. 1830)

A charming cottage on the outskirts of Dungarvan enhances the character of the area.

BALLEIGHTERAGH EAST
(c. 1800)

The survival of most of the original fabric enhances the picturesque quality of this cottage.

Although there are many attractive examples across the county, Waterford's stock of small vernacular housing is much depleted. Nonetheless examples survive to provide an indication of the quality and merit of a once ubiquitous housing type. As with all vernacular buildings these houses, together with their outbuildings, employed readily available building materials, from what would now be defined as renewable sources. Many of the vernacular cottages in the county were thatched with reed harvested from the banks of the Blackwater and the Suir. Employing simple forms and bright colours, they sat comfortably in the landscape and generally benefited from a placement which ensured shelter from prevailing winds. Some surviving examples embellished in the nineteenth century actually date back to the previous period and include houses such as that at Garraun (c. 1760) *(fig. 165)*. It is readily apparent that the house originally consisted of the central three-bay component and has

(fig. 165)
GARRAUN
(c. 1760)

Features such as the long low massing, the diminutive proportions to the openings, and the thatched roof all typify the vernacular tradition in County Waterford. The cottage was well restored in the 1980s and retains much of its picturesque character.

BALLINGOWAN EAST
(c. 1830)

This cottage, in common with many of the vernacular cottages in the county, was traditionally thatched with reed gleaned from the banks of the Suir and Blackwater rivers. Most of the reed now used in thatching is imported.

been enlarged over the decades. It was sensitively restored in 1985 and is supported by a range of outbuildings that have been well maintained over the years. Other examples providing evidence of an incremental enlargement include a house at Garranturton (c. 1790). As with all of these houses, windows were added at date later than the actual construction; we can find examples with mid-nineteenth century sash windows and others with windows dating from the early twentieth century. In most such cases it is noteworthy that the alterations sit comfortably with the original form of the house. Other well-maintained houses in this tradition include examples at Garrarus (c. 1800) *(figs. 166 - 167)* and Ballynakill (c. 1820) *(fig. 168)*. Vernacular modes were also commonplace for residences at the heart of larger farms; here again it is possible to discern the employment of simple forms and readily available materials, as at Dromore Cottage (c. 1820) *(fig. 169)*. Other detached farmhouses of the period, like that at Curraheenavoher (c. 1850), still retained vernacular lines even when rendered and benefiting from slate roofs, indica-

(fig. 166)
GARRARUS
(c. 1800)

The evolution of this cottage over time is evident in the variations of each additional range; the limewashed rubble stone construction and slate roof to the end bay, and the corrugated-iron roof to the porch.

(fig. 167)
GARRARUS

Margined timber sash windows lend a formal tone to the vernacular quality of the cottage.

(fig. 168)
BALLYNAKILL
(c. 1820)

Ballynakill provides a well-maintained example of the vernacular heritage of County Waterford.

Regular proportions and margined timber sash windows contribute an elegant quality to this prominently sited thatched cottage.

(fig. 169)
DROMORE COTTAGE
Dromore
(c. 1820)

Measuring over one hundred feet in length, this long low range incorporates a farmhouse and outbuildings in a single integrated structure.
The cottage forms part of an extensive agricultural complex of vernacular importance.

BALLINATTIN
(c. 1850)

An attractive cottage appears to mould into the landscape as a result of the stepping down of one bay.

KNOCKALISHEEN
(c. 1800)

A small scale farmhouse and associated outbuilding ranges produce a picturesque ensemble of vernacular importance.

(fig. 170)
CURRAHEENAVOHER
(c. 1850)

The modestly scaled farmhouse of some formal quality shows balanced proportions and Classical symmetry; the outbuildings introduce an element of the vernacular and are constructed from unrefined materials in an unconsciously designed manner.

tive at the time as a major improvement in the social status of the owner *(fig. 170)*. In addition the preferred option of centrally placed doorways and motifs such as architraves reveal the legacy of the Classical architectural tradition. This is especially evident in farmhouses such as Niervale House (c. 1880) at Ballymacarbry. The villa-like appearance of the main farmhouse, three bays with central doorway, was of a type that became quite widespread across Ireland both in rural and suburban housing *(fig. 171)*. The farm at Niervale also benefits from an attractive array of fine outbuildings (c.1880) *(figs. 172 - 173)*. The Classical influence is even more apparent in larger farmhouses like Brook Lodge (c. 1850) *(fig. 174)*. The forms and building materials employed in the vernacular tradition continued to be employed, or maintained in the case of existing buildings, well into the twentieth century.

(fig. 171)
NIERVALE (HOUSE)
Ballymacarbry
(c. 1880)

A medium sized villa-style house forms the centrepiece of an extensive farmyard complex. Stone cobbling to the courtyard enhances the setting of the site.

(fig. 172)
NIERVALE (HOUSE)
Ballymacarbry

The large scale outbuildings accommodate a wide range of farm-related activities and include stable blocks, coach houses, and barns.

(fig. 173)
NIERVALE (HOUSE)
Ballymacarbry

A window opening in the stable building retains its original timber joinery and early glazing.

GARRARUS
(c. 1825)

The informal appearance and construction in unrefined materials identify the vernacular significance of such rural outbuildings.

(fig. 174)
BROOK LODGE
Brooklodge
(c. 1850)

Balanced proportions, subtle architectural features, and minimal extraneous ornamentation produce a typical farmhouse of functional appearance; the onerous task of working the land left little opportunity to spend resources on outstanding architectural inventions.

The Twentieth Century

(fig. 175)
PLUNKETT
RAILWAY STATION
(WATERFORD (NORTH)
RAILWAY STATION)
Terminus Street,
Waterford
(c. 1930)

A timber clad signal
box spans the railway
line; a hut positioned on
a platform is the more
familiar form.

The new century opened with the promise of technological improvement and the anticipation of reform, offset by a serious decline in trade, industry, and agriculture. Social and political change were hastened through a series of traumatic events, most notably the advent of World War I (1914-18), and with even more dramatic consequence for Waterford, the Easter Uprising (1916), the formation of Dáil Éireann (1919), the Anglo-Irish Treaty (1921) and the following Civil War (1921-23). Changes in the political structures often first became apparent in matters of detail rather than overall architectural innovation. Surviving post boxes provide indicators of such change and the county retains post boxes with the monogram ER VII for King Edward VII at Adamstown (c. 1905); GR for King George V at Glennanore (c. 1915); and SÉ for Saorsat Éireann at Farnane Upper (c. 1930). In spite of these political changes and challenges, affecting all areas of Waterford, developments continued apace, if sometimes sporadically. In many respects, economic deprivation and at later periods in the century

what might be seen as economic stagnation, helped to preserve and maintain the fabric of towns and villages. It was only from the 1960s onwards that serious threats were posed to old streets, shopfronts, and churches, to name but a few. Most of the changes to the architectural fabric of Portlaw date from the second half of the century, resulting in the disappearance of half of the housing in the original 'Model' town.

In the early years of the century, with private motorised transport confined to the rich, the railway system could afford to develop further. In Waterford City, a new train station, now Plunkett Station, (1908), across Edmund Rice Bridge, brought the railway to the actual gateway of the city and afforded travellers and locals alike an impressive vista of the riverside city as they disembarked. The line had previously terminated at Dunkitt, with southward lines departing from a station on Manor Street. Ranges of features survive from this time, such as the signal box (rebuilt c. 1930) *(fig. 175)* spanning the line on its metal support frame

(fig. 176)
1-7 WESTERN TERRACE
Old Chapel Lane,
Dungarvan
(1910)

A group of seven identical units, each house containing distinctive qualities such as recessed façades, bay windows, paired window openings, balconies, and simple iron railings.

(fig. 177)
11-12 ALEXANDER STREET
Waterford
(1910)

One of a group of seven units accommodating a separate apartment on each floor, as indicated in the illustration by the different colours applied to the windows. Of the group, this example is the last to retain the original materials in their entirety.

and the elongated platform canopy (1908). Improvements to the railway lines elsewhere in the country included the significant span of Suir Bridge (1906) at Cheekpoint.

The necessity for publicly funded housing schemes was pressing. Built with limited economic resources, such schemes would not meet the standards or tastes of today; nevertheless they were generally well designed. By necessity architectural embellishment was kept to the minimum. Waterford County Council developed a number of projects including a well-designed range of houses in Western Terrace (1910), Old Chapel Lane, Dungarvan *(fig. 176)*. Number 5 Western Terrace has retained much of its original fabric, door, metal railings, and windows. As was formerly the case in many Irish towns, rows of small-single storey houses line the roads that approach the town. A row of some eighteen houses on O'Connell Street (c. 1900) terminates at either end in two-storey houses akin to 'book-ends'. Public housing initiatives in Waterford City included a group of seven houses (1910) on a restricted site on steep Alexander Street, each accommodating two residential units. Numbers 11 and 12 Alexander Street have been well maintained and retain their original fittings *(fig. 177)*. Rusticated cut-stone lintels set against the plain rendered walls add character to these buildings.

Private philanthropy continued and the Carnegie Free Libraries (1905-11) throughout the county bear witness to the munificence of Scots-born philanthropist Andrew Carnegie (1835-1919). As with their equivalent libraries in the United States of America and New Zealand, the varied library buildings subscribe to certain design guidelines, both internally and externally. Their civic purpose was hinted at through decorative, if not extravagant, exteriors. Architectural detail was at best eclectic and sufficient to reflect favourably on the espoused noble purpose of the building. The prominently sited library (1903-05) on Lady Lane, Waterford City, was designed in an understated Classical idiom by Albert Edward Murray (1849-1924); Andrew Carnegie himself visited the city to lay the foundation stone. The library (opened 1911) in Cappoquin was designed by George P. Sheridan (d. 1950) and reveals the influence of Arts and Crafts with the Queen Anne Revival style, popular at the turn of the century *(fig. 178)*.

(fig. 179)
81-84 COAL QUAY
Waterford
(1905)

A group of four identical buildings were built to house a commercial space in the ground floor with residential accommodation over. Robust rendered dressings contribute to the quality of the design and enhance the impact of the group in the streetscape.

(fig. 178)
CAPPOQUIN CARNEGIE
FREE LIBRARY
Main Street,
Cappoquin
(opened 1911)

The Scottish-American industrialist Andrew Carnegie (1835-1919) sponsored five libraries in County Waterford; each is stylistically distinctive. The library at Cappoquin juxtaposes motifs of the Queen Anne and the Arts and Crafts movements.

(fig. 180)
THE BANK
Gladstone Street/
O'Connell Street,
Waterford
(c. 1910)

The design of the bank has been carefully considered to maximise the potential of the important corner site. Almost identical façades face on to each street, with a central entrance bay vigorously articulated in a Classical manner.

(fig. 181)
CUSTOM HOUSE QUAY
Waterford
(c. 1910)

Following the conversion
of the quays to use as a
car park in the 1980s, a
steel crane, one of a pair
remaining in the city,
survives as an artefact of
the industrial legacy of
Waterford.

Commercial buildings continued to espouse Classicism well into the century, if sometimes with a gusto and vibrancy of detail previously lacking. In Waterford some quayside houses were replaced, or enhanced with decorative detailing. A new terrace of four (1905) was erected on Coal Quay where many Classical details remain as evidence of aspirations of grandeur *(fig. 179)*. The former bank (c. 1910) on the corner of Gladstone and O'Connell Streets takes advantage of its corner site to benefit from a chamfered entrance bay *(fig. 180)*. It provides a comparative wealth of Classical detailing with the pedimented doorcase and upper storey bay windows flanked by Ionic columns, the whole supporting a pediment and entablature in turn surmounted by an attic. The ongoing importance of Waterford's maritime tradition, and its wealth of river borne trade, was reflected in developments on or near the quays, including those of a technical nature without, or with only minimal, references to architectural precedents. The large freestanding steel crane (c. 1910) on Custom House Quay, complete with its original mechanism, is one of a pair in the city *(figs. 181 - 182)*. The Granary (1905), built for R. and H.

(fig. 182)
CUSTOM HOUSE QUAY
Waterford

The juxtaposition of steel
beams and lattice girders
adds an almost sculptural
quality to the
streetscape.

(fig. 184)
CAPPOQUIN HOUSE
Cappoquin Demesne,
Cappoquin
(1779 and post-1925)

The ancestral home of
the Keane family, the
house was destroyed
during 'The Troubles'
(1922-3). Subsequently
rebuilt, the original
entrance front, pictured,
was reordered as the
Garden Front overlooking
the River Blackwater.

(fig. 183)
R. AND H. HALL
FLOUR MILLS
Dock Road,
Waterford
(1905)

Upon completion,
the warehouse stood as
an architectural gate-
crasher against the back-
drop of the eighteent-
and nineteenth-century
streetscapes of the quays
on the opposite side
of the river. Over the
century, however, much
of the dramatic impact
of the starkly Modernist
design has been dimin-
ished by the develop-
ment of the adjacent
sites.

*Courtesy of the National
Library of Ireland.*

Hall flour millers was designed by the engineer W. Friel *(fig. 183)*. Built of reinforced concrete, this nine-storey structure was radically different to any large-scale building previously erected in the city. Its construction followed the Hennebique system devised by the pioneering French architect Francois Hennebique (1842-1921). The simple cubic form underscores its purpose and method of construction, and the severity is only relieved by the punctuation of windows and minimal relief decoration. The buildings erected around the same period on the site of Cherry's Brewery (c. 1905), Mary Street, a centre of brewing since the early eighteenth century, were equally pragmatic. Although the complex is now disused, it retains on site the machinery associated with brewing.

The political unrest of the War of Independence and the Civil War resulted in the destruction of buildings, public and private, across the county. However, in contrast with neighbouring County Cork, comparatively few large houses were destroyed outright. Of those that were damaged many were rebuilt; Gardenmorris (originally c. 1820), burnt in 1923, was subsequently recreated. The late eighteenth-century Cappoquin House (original-ly 1779), home of the Keane Family, was also burnt in 1923 but was reconstructed with great care to designs by Richard Orpen (1863-1938), brother of the more famous society painter William (1878-1931) *(fig. 184)*. The by-then conservative aesthetic in which Cappoquin was rebuilt underlined the cautious approach to architecture that more or less dominated the century. The extensive remodelling and embellishment of Mount Congreve (originally c. 1750), Kilmeadan, in the mid-1960s took a similarly cautious, if not inappropriate, approach.

Few buildings that could be called Modernist were erected. In Ireland, as elsewhere, motifs from current fashion were frequently employed in elevations and decorative detailing, while little change was instigated in the interior planning which remained at best conventional. That is not to say that alterations and extensions did not embrace technical innovations. Public architecture, including hospitals and schools, frequently shows some of the first evidence of such change. An observation post (c. 1940) erected during Second World War (1939-45) was constructed in mass-concrete, and together with school shelters and ball alleys, was as brutalist and severe as might be expected in any such structure *(fig. 185)*.

(fig. 185)
DYSERT
(c. 1940)

A relic of the measures put in place during 'The Emergency' (1939-45), the construction of the watch tower in mass concrete produces a brutalist, functional appearance that is in contrast with the picturesque value of the earlier tower nearby.

Burke's (c. 1940) on O'Connell Street, Waterford, erected in this period of great austerity, is a pared-down example of a Moderne style that reveals an awareness of current international trends, at least on its façade. The building's stepped red brick and roughcast walls, all given strong horizontality through the wide ground floor display windows and steel-framed windows above, must have appeared shockingly innovative in its day. The glass block sections inserted into the ground floor piers allude to Modernist influence. Unencumbered by the past and with references from across the world, cinema architecture was among the most confident in embracing a new aesthetic, even if this too was frequently only expressed in matters of decoration and detailing. The Ormonde Cinema (c. 1945), O'Connell Street, Dungarvan, was redolent of modernity and of the cinema age, if not quite of Modernism, which is altogether more severe and yet refined *(fig. 186)*. The combination of elements on the well-proportioned façade such as the stepped roofline, horizontal banding, and windows, suggested a world of glamour and escapism only to be matched by the confections on the screen. It is worth noting how the lighting of the façade would have added greatly to its original impact. New shopfronts, from the middle of the century onwards, frequently emulated such glamour, if on a smaller scale, through employing polished chrome decoration and stylish lettering. Like some architectural 'Brylcreem' the emphasis was on looking smart and slick. A prominently sited commercial property (rebuilt c. 1950), Grattan Square, Dungarvan, employed a black resin compound cladding at shopfront level. Horizontal banding and a stepped parapet

added to the sense of distinction that set the shop apart from, but not in battle with, more traditional fronts. The new industrial blocks erected in the post war period at the disused cotton mill at Portlaw were more rigorously Modernist. The leather tanning works was launched in 1945 and remained in business until the 1980s. The massive plant erected at that time survives, if dilapidated, with its monumental concrete frame proclaiming loudly, as few buildings did in Ireland at the time, its embrace of Modernism. The corrugated canopy at one end recalls Michael Scott's (1905-88) contemporary work at Busáras, Dublin (completed 1953).

(fig. 186)
ORMONDE CINEMA
O'Connell Street/
Stephen's Street,
Dungarvan
(c. 1945)

The Ormonde is typical of many such cinemas constructed in Ireland in the mid twentieth century. A frontage of Modernist aspirations incorporating clean bold horizontal lines screens an auditorium of minimal architectural pretension. The coloured glass panels to the first floor contribute to the design quality of the site.

(fig. 188)
WATERFORD
BAPTIST CHURCH
Catherine Street,
Waterford

Panels of yellow terracotta
featuring a foliate motif
provide subtle decorative
incident to the design.

(fig. 187)
WATERFORD
BAPTIST CHURCH
Catherine Street,
Waterford
(1910)

A small scale church is
given prominence in the
streetscape through a
construction in red brick
with limestone ashlar horizontal bands, the vertical
emphasis of the openings,
and a battlemented para-
pet. The church is similar
to Dutch and Flemish
public buildings of the
early twentieth century.

Architecture for places of worship remained
firmly in the embrace of traditional forms and
ideas well into the century. Indeed the new
church (1910) built for the growing Baptist
community in Waterford recalled the mid nineteenth century with its Ruskin-inspired polychrome bands of red brick and cream limestone, the whole counteracted by the vertical
thrust of five lancet windows, offset with yellow terracotta panels (figs. 187 - 188). More
spectacularly, it was only in the 1920s that the

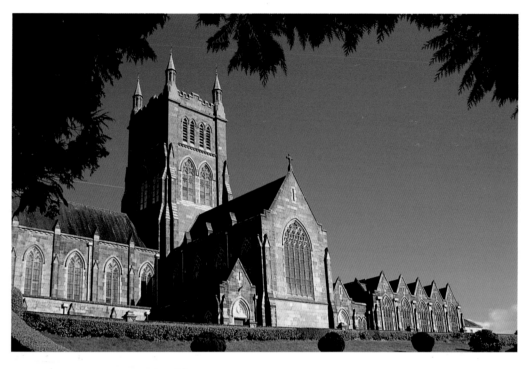

(fig. 189)
MOUNT MELLERAY
MONASTERY
Mountmelleray
(c. 1925)

A monumental abbey church in a solid muscular Gothic Revival style, built to designs prepared by Alfred Jones (1822-1925), uses limestone salvaged from Mitchelstown Castle, County Cork. The building sits in a relatively empty landscape and forms a dramatic visual incident.

Interior of Church, Mount Melleray Abbey, Co. Waterford.

(fig. 190)
MOUNT MELLERARY
MONASTERY
Mountmelleray

An archival view of the expansive interior of the abbey church illustrates a groin-vaulted ceiling that is comparable with Saint Carthage's Cathedral, Lismore. The timber pews and panelled walls are indicative of high quality timber joinery.

Courtesy of the Irish Architectural Archive.

great Abbey Church at Mount Melleray (c. 1925), Cappoquin, was completed *(figs. 189 - 190)*. True to the Cistercian architectural tradition it is a severe but hugely impressive building with a clear massing of elements. Its great looming pinnacled tower is a distinctive feature on the skyline for miles around. Modern styles were adopted in the building of Catholic churches from the 1950s on, and even where elements of Classicism or Gothicism remained they were interpreted in a spare manner that clearly proclaimed twentieth century taste. The Catholic Church of the Sacred Heart (1973) on Lower Grange Road, Waterford, is indicative of the transformation in church architecture from the 1960s *(fig. 191)*. Placed on a corner site, the church was designed on an octagonal plan with a stepped roof. This central emphasis echoed the interior of church, where the altar was placed on a raised sanctuary at the centre of the airy full height interior. The longitudinal axis that had dominated church planning for centuries had been shifted radically — an alteration that reflected changes in liturgical practice as well as architectural innovation.

(fig. 191)
CATHOLIC CHURCH OF THE SACRED HEART
Richardson's Folly/ Lower Grange Road, Waterford
(1973)

The use of radical architectural styles and planning formulae was officially sanctioned following the Second Vatican Council (1963-5) and resulted in inventive schemes such as C. Harvey Jacob's polygonal composition, distinguished by a stepped profile to the roof incorporating prominent concrete ribs.

Conclusion

(fig. 192)
KILLOTERAN CHURCH
Killoteran
(c. 1860)

Having experienced a
decline in fortune in the
mid twentieth century
this church was success-
fully converted to an
alternative use in 1999.
The building retains most
of its original character
while serving as a
reminder of the once
prosperous Church of
Ireland community in
the locality.

County Waterford has enjoyed a period of increased prosperity in the late twentieth century, although changing employment patterns and altered modes of agricultural production have not been without their own challenges, with consequences, in particular, for rural settlements and small villages. While Waterford City has experienced continued expansion, rural urban areas such as Cappoquin and Lismore are more or less defined by a historic core that has changed little over the past one hundred years. Similarly much of the outlying areas retain their rural character — a journey through the county typically features urban areas and clusters linked by long sections of countryside experiencing minimal building activity. Happily, the coastline of the county retains its rugged charm.

Of late there is a welcome growing awareness of the built legacy of earlier generations, and of buildings as signifiers of the ebb and flow of the county's fortunes. Many fine buildings remain and have been adapted for present-day use. The Assembly Buildings on The Mall fulfil a civic function still at the heart of Waterford City while the Granary on Merchant's Quay looks to the future while preserving the city's past. The former town hall (1861), on Friary Street, Dungarvan, has been successfully converted to use as an award-winning museum while retaining the early character of the site. More than half of the houses that formed the 'Model' village at Portlaw have disappeared but the county council has built houses (c. 1940) there with a regularity of form and appearance that continues the planned character of the area. Nearby the small Gothic Revival church, Killoteran (c. 1860) has been sympathetically converted (1999) to residential use *(fig. 192)*. The gate lodge at Salterbridge House, Cappoquin (1849) has been fully restored for the Irish Landmark Trust.

Progress is often seen to be best served by an embrace of something new and an abandonment of something old, be it a building itself, or its details — the windows, the original render on a street front or the old shopfront. So much can be reutilised and adapted. This not only has the benefit of reflecting principles of sustainability and recycling, but also provides a direct visual link with the cultures and people who have gone before us.

The range of artefacts, buildings, and structures covered in this Introduction constitutes but a small portion of the architectural heritage of County Waterford. The NIAH County Survey has identified a wide range of structures of importance, from public buildings such as banks, churches, courthouses, and market houses, to private projects such as cottages,

houses and farm buildings. The survival of buildings from the periods covered by the survey (post 1700) is testimony to the durability of construction and design with which they were conceived.

The architectural fabric of previous centuries is among the most tangible evidence providing insight into the history of a county. As history is continuously being written it will be necessary to examine and re-assess the architectural legacy of the twentieth century, as the buildings of that period will, in turn, represent the architectural heritage for future generations. The architecture of the past is a legacy to the present. So too the architecture of the present will represent a legacy to the future of the culture and ideals of the people of County Waterford.

Further Reading

Aalen, F.H.A., Whelan Kevin
and Stout, Matthew, eds.,
Atlas of the Irish
Rural Landscape
(Cork: Cork University
Press, 1997)

Bence-Jones, Mark,
A Guide to Irish
Country Houses
(London: Constable Press, 1988)

Casserley, H.C.,
Outline of Irish
Railway History
(London: David &
Charles, 1974)

Cowman, Des,
The Role of Waterford
Chamber of Commerce
1787-1987
(Waterford: Waterford Chamber
of Commerce 1988).

Craig, Maurice,
Classic Irish Houses
of the Middle Size
(London: Architectural
Press, 1976).

Craig, Maurice and
Garner, William,
'Revised Report on areas and
sites of historical and artistic
interest in Co. Waterford'
(Dublin: National Institute
for Physical Planning and
Constructive Research, 1977)

Craig, Maurice,
The Architecture of Ireland
from the earliest times to 1880
(London: Batsford, Dublin:
Eason, 1989).

Dowling, Daniel,
Waterford Streets:
Past and Present
(Waterford: Waterford
Corporation, 1998).

Dunne, Mildred,
and Phillips, Brian,
Courthouses of Ireland: A
gazetteer of Irish Courthouses
(Kilkenny: The Heritage
Council, 1999).

Egan, P.M.,
History, Guide and Directory
of the County and City of
Waterford
(Kilkenny: 1895).

Fayle, H and Newham, A.T.,
The Waterford and Tramore
Railway
(London: David &
Charles, 1964)

Foster, Roy E., ed.,
The Oxford Illustrated
History of Ireland
(London: BCA by arrangement
with Oxford University
Press, 1989).

Fraher, William,
Guide to Historic Dungarvan
(Dungarvan: Dungarvan
Museum Society, 1991)

Garner, William,
'Revised Report on buildings
of architectural interest in
Waterford City'
(Dublin: National Institute for
Physical Planning and
Constructive Research, 1983)

Girouard, Mark,
'Curraghmore, Co. Waterford'
(Country Life, cxxxiii, nos.
3440-2, 1963 pp.256-60,
308-11, 368-71).

Girouard, Mark,
'Lismore Castle, Co. Waterford'
(Country Life, cxxxvi, nos.
3518-19, pp.336-40, 389-93).

Girouard, Mark,
Town and Country
(New Haven & London:
Yale University Press, 1992)

Grimes, Brendan,
Irish Carnegie Free Libraries
(Dublin: Irish Academic
Press, 1998).

Hunt, Tom,
Portlaw, Co. Waterford
1825-76: portrait of an
industrial village
(Dublin: Irish Academic
Press, 2000).

Howley, James,
The Follies and Garden
Buildings of Ireland
(New Haven and London:
Yale University Press, 1993).

Lohan, Rena,
Guide to the Archives of
The Office of Public Works
(Dublin: Stationery
Office, 1994).

Lumley, Ian W. J.,
'The Georgian Townhouses
of Waterford: an architectural
Assessment'
(Decies: Old Waterford Society
Journal, xxxiv, 1987)

McParland, Edward,
James Gandon Vitruvius
Hibernicus
(London: A. Zwemmer, 1985).

McParland, Edward,
Public Architecture
In Ireland 1680-1760
(New Haven & London:
Yale University Press, 2001).

Miley, G., Cronin, J.,
Sleeman, M., et al.,
Heritage Conservation Plan
Portlaw County Waterford
(Kilkenny: The Heritage
Council, 2003).

Moore, Michael,
Archaeological Inventory of
County Waterford
(Dublin: The Stationary
Office, 1999).

Nolan, William and Power,
Thomas, eds.,
Waterford History and Society
(Dublin: Geography
Publications, 1998).

Rothery, Sean,
A Field Guide to the
Buildings of Ireland
(Dublin: The Lilliput
Press, 1997).

Ryland, Rev. R.H.,
History, Topography and
Antiquities of Co. and
City of Waterford
(London: John Murray, 1824).

Smith, Charles,
Antient and Present
State of the County and
City of Waterford
(Cork: 1746).

Williams, Jeremy,
Companion Guide to
Architecture in Ireland
1837-1921
(Dublin: Irish Academic
Press, 1994).

Registration Numbers

The structures mentioned in the text of this Introduction are listed below. It is possible to find more information on each structure by searching the NIAH databases by the Registration Number.

03 Pier, Villierstown Td.,
Villierstown
Reg. 22819013

05 Reginald's Tower, Parade
Quay/The Mall, Waterford City
Td., Waterford
Not included in survey

05 Tower Hotel, The Mall,
Waterford
Not included in survey

07 Mill, Ballydowane West Td.
Not included in survey

07 Ardmore Cathedral,
Ardocheasty Td./Monea Td.,
Ardmore
Not included in survey

07 Saint Mochuda's Cathedral,
North Mall, Lismore (Cos. By.)
Td., Lismore
Now gone

08 Reginald's Tower, Parade
Quay/The Mall, Waterford City
Td., Waterford
Not included in survey

08 Dungarvan Castle, Davitt's
Quay/Castle Street, Dungarvan
Td., Dungarvan
Not included in survey

08 Dungarvan Market House,
Main Street (Parnell
Street)/Castle Street/Quay
Street, Dungarvan Td.,
Dungarvan
Reg. 22821147

08 Citadel (The), Waterford City
Td., Waterford
Now gone

09 Tikincor Castle,
Tikincor Lower Td.
Not included in survey

09 Castle Farm (Ballyduff Castle),
Ballyduff Lower Td., Ballyduff
Reg. 22808013

09 Lismore Castle, Lismore
(Cos. By.) Td., Lismore
Reg. 22809079

09 Gardens, Lismore Castle,
Lismore (Cos. By.) Td., Lismore
Reg. 22809071

10-12 Ballygunner Castle,
Ballygunnercastle Td.
Reg. 22901816

10 Riding House (The), Lismore
Castle, Castle Avenue, Lismore
(Cos. By.) Td., Lismore
Reg. 22809070

11 Castle Dodard,
Knockaungarriff Td.
Reg. 22901201

11 Mount Odell (House),
Mountodell Td.
Reg. 22903031

11-12 Glenbeg House, Glen Beg
(Cos. By.) Td.
Reg. 22902002

12-13 Newtown House, Newtown
(Mid. By.) Drumcannon
Par. Td.
Reg. 22902606

13 Mill, Ballycanvan Big Td.,
Spring Hill
Not included in survey

14-15 Villierstown Church,
Villierstown Td., Villierstown
Reg. 22819003

15-16 Dromana House, Dromana
(D. Wt. By.) Td.
Reg. 22902918

17 The Bastions, Dromana House,
Dromana (D. Wt. By.) Td.
Reg. 22902917

18 Tallow Bridge, Tallowbridge
Lands Td./Townparks East
(Cos. By.) Tallow Par. Td.,
Tallowbridge
Reg. 22902806

18 Knocklofty Bridge,
Kilnamack West
Reg. 22900104

18 Strand Bridge, Ballyin Lower
Td./Ballyrafter Td./Ballyrafter
Flats Td., Lismore
Reg. 22809083

18 'Timber Toes' Bridge, Waterford
City Td., Waterford
Now gone

18 Edmund Rice Bridge, Waterford
City Td., Waterford
Reg. 22500075

18-19 Waterford Military Barracks,
Barrack Street/Green
Street/Newport Square,
Waterford City Td., Waterford
*Reg. 22502156, 22502540,
22502543, 22502989*

18-19 Soldier's Homes, Waterford
Military Barracks, Green Street,
Waterford City Td., Waterford
Reg. 22502543

19 Dungarvan Military Barracks,
Dungarvan Castle, Davitt's
Quay/Castle Street, Dungarvan
Td., Dungarvan
Not included in survey

19-20 New Geneva Barracks,
Newtown (Gaul. By.)
Crooke Par. Td.
Reg. 22901810

20 Reginald's Tower, Parade
Quay/The Mall, Waterford City
Td., Waterford
Not included in survey

21-22 Deanery (The), Cathedral
Square/Bailey's New Street,
Waterford City Td., Waterford
Reg. 22504096

22 5 O'Connell Street, Waterford
City Td., Waterford
Reg. 22500306

22 Ozanam House, 18 Lady Lane,
Waterford City Td., Waterford
Reg. 22504355

22-23 Waterford Vocational
Educational Committee,
30 The Mall, Waterford City
Td., Waterford
Reg. 22504328

22-23 Waterford Bishop's Palace,
The Mall. Waterford City Td.,
Waterford
Reg. 22504094

24 Saint Patrick's Methodist and
Presbyterian Church, Patrick
Street, Waterford City Td.,
Waterford
Reg. 22501448

24 Saint Patrick's Catholic Church,
Jenkin's Lane, Waterford City
Td., Waterford
Reg. 22501489

25-27 Curraghmore House,
Curraghmore Td.
Reg. 22900816

28-29 ChristChurch Cathedral,
Cathedral Square, Waterford
City Td., Waterford
Reg. 22504095

29 Catholic Cathedral of the Holy
Trinity, Barronstrand Street,
Waterford City Td., Waterford
Reg. 22501138

30-31 Waterford Town Hall and
Theatre Royal, The Mall,
Waterford City Td., Waterford
Reg. 22504135

32-33 Waterford Chamber of
Commerce/Port of Waterford
Company (Morris House),
2 Great George's Street,
Waterford City Td., Waterford
Reg. 22501514

34-35 Canal, Kilbree East Td./Kilbree West Td./Ballyea East Td./Ballyea West Td./Ballynelligan Glebe Td./Lismore (Cos. By.) Td./Ballyrafter Flats Td./Ballynadeige Td./Salterbridge Td./Fadduaga Td./Cappoquin Demesne Td., Cappoquin and Lismore
Not included in survey

34-35 Daisybank House, Cheekpoint Td., Cheekpoint
Reg. 22901006

34-36 Dunmore East Harbour, Dunmore Bay, Dunmore Td., Dunmore East
Reg. 22817064

34-36 Dunmore Harbour House, Dock Road, Dunmore Td., Dunmore East
Reg. 22817065

34-36 Dunmore East Lighthouse, Dunmore Bay, Dunmore Td., Dunmore East
Reg. 22817063

35 Cappoquin Railway Viaduct, Kilbree East Td./Cappoquin Td., Cappoquin
Reg. 22810114

36-37 Metal Man Tower (The), Westtown Td.
Reg. 22902605

36-38 Ardmore Head Watch Tower, Dysert Td.
Reg. 22904006

38 Mine Head Lighthouse, Monagoush Td.
Reg. 22903904

39 Lighthouse Keeper's Cottage, Mine Head Lighthouse, Monagoush Td.
Reg. 22903905, 22903906

39 Milestone, Red Forge Crossroads, Garryduff (Cos. By.) Td.
Reg. 22903719

39 Causeway Bridge, Abbeyside Td./Dungarvan Td., Dungarvan
Reg. 22821014

39 Barnawee Bridge, Duckspool Td./Kilminnin North Td./Kilminnin South Td.
Reg. 22903108

39 Little Bridge, Cappoquin Td./Littlebridge Inches Td./Kilderriheen Td., Cappoquin
Reg. 22810054

40-41 Cavendish Bridge (Lismore Bridge), Ballyin Lower Td./Ballyrafter Flats Td./Lismore (Cos. By.) Td., Lismore
Reg. 22809082

40-41 Ballyduff Bridge, Ballyduff (Cos. By.) Td./Garrison Td./Ballyduff Lower Td., Ballyduff
Reg. 22808002

40 Tramore Railway Station, Turkey Road/Lower Branch Road, Tramore East Td., Tramore
Reg. 22816111

40 Railway Goods Shed, Lismore Railway Station, Railway Road, Townparks East (Cos. By.) Lism. Par. Td., Lismore
Reg. 22809154

40 Tramore Railway Station, Railway Road, Townparks East (Cos. By.) Lism. Par. Td., Lismore
Reg. 22809062

40 Ballyvoyle Railway Tunnel, Ballyvoyle Td.
Reg. 22903207

40-42 Kilmacthomas Railway Viaduct, Kilmacthomas Td., Kilmacthomas
Reg. 22805032

40-42 Mahon Railway Viaduct, Graigueshoneen Td./Kilmacthomas Td., Kilmacthomas
Reg. 22805035

42 Kilmacthomas Railway Station, Kilmacthomas Td., Kilmacthomas
Reg. 22805044

42 Cappoquin Railway Station, Cook Street (off), Cappoquin Td., Cappoquin
Reg. 22810053

42 Railway Goods Shed, Cappoquin Railway Station, Cook Street (off), Cappoquin Td., Cappoquin
Reg. 22810107

42 Water Tower, Cappoquin Railway Station, Cook Street (off), Cappoquin Td., Cappoquin
Reg. 22810108

42 Signal Box, Cappoquin Railway Station, Cook Street (off), Cappoquin Td., Cappoquin
Reg. 22810106

43 Ballyvoyle Railway Viaduct, Ballyvoyle Td./Knockyoolahan East Td.
Reg. 22903205

43 Tramore Railway Station, Railway Road, Townparks East (Cos. By.) Lism. Par. Td., Lismore
Reg. 22809062

44 Ambrose Power Memorial Fountain, The Square, Lismore (Cos. By.) Td., Lismore
Reg. 22809033

44-45 Waterpump, The Green, Villierstown Td., Villierstown
Reg. 22819008

44 Estate Worker's House, New Street, Lismore (Cos. By.) Td., Lismore
Reg. 22809042

45 Lismore Arms Hotel, Main Street/The Square, Lismore (Cos. By.) Td., Lismore
Reg. 22809001

45 Red House Inn (The), Main Street/Chapel Street, Lismore (Cos. By.) Td., Lismore
Reg. 22809032

45 Lismore Courthouse, West Street/Chapel Street, Lismore (Cos. By.) Td., Lismore
Reg. 22809034

47 Grendon (House), Dock Road, Dunmore Td., Dunmore East
Reg. 22817031

47 Hook View (House), Dock Road, Dunmore Td., Dunmore East
Reg. 22817032

47 Sunrise Cottage, Dock Road, Dunmore Td., Dunmore East
Reg. 22817033

47 Loftus View (House), Dock Road, Dunmore Td., Dunmore East
Reg. 22817034

47 Woodville (House), Dock Road, Dunmore Td., Dunmore East
Reg. 22817035

47 Thatched Cottage, Dock Road, Dunmore Td., Dunmore East
Reg. 22817036

47-49 Seaview Cottage, Dock Road, Dunmore Td., Dunmore East
Reg. 22817037

49 Crab Cottage, Dock Road, Dunmore Td., Dunmore East
Reg. 22817038

49 Thatched Cottage, Dock Road, Dunmore Td., Dunmore East
Reg. 22817039

49 Haven Hotel (Villa Marina), Dock Road, Dunmore Td., Dunmore East
Reg. 22817021

49 Lismore Arms Hotel, Main Street/The Square, Lismore (Cos. By.) Td., Lismore
Reg. 22809001

49 Moore's Hotel, Main Street, Cappoquin Td., Cappoquin
Reg. 22810064 - 22810065

49 2 King's Terrace, Waterford City Td., Waterford
Reg. 22502304

49 3 King's Terrace, Waterford City Td., Waterford
Reg. 22502305

49 4 King's Terrace, Waterford City Td., Waterford
Reg. 22502306

49 5 King's Terrace, Waterford City Td., Waterford
Reg. 22502307

49 House, Barrack Street, Passage East Td., Passage East
Reg. 22807042

49 Passage East Garda Síochána Station, Barrack Street, Passage East Td., Passage East
Reg. 22807043

50 Courthouse and School, Factory Road (off), Coolroe (Upp. By.) Clonagam Par. Td., Portlaw
Reg. 22803055

50 Lismore Courthouse, West Street/Chapel Street, Lismore (Cos. By.) Td., Lismore
Reg. 22809034

50 Dungarvan Courthouse, Meagher Street, Dungarvan Td., Dungarvan
Reg. 22821019

50-51 Waterford Courthouse, Catherine Street, Waterford City Td., Waterford
Reg. 22504492

52 Ballyduff Garda Síochána Station, Ballyduff Lower Td., Ballyduff
Reg. 22808001

52-53 Castlerichard School, Glencairn Td., Castlerichard
Reg. 22902010

52-53 Scoil Cluain Fiaid Paorac Scoil Náisiúnta, Ballyneal Td., Clonea
Reg. 22802011

52-53 Glennawillin National School, Glennawillin Crossroads, Glennawillin Td., Glennawillin
Reg. 22902801

54 Carrignagower National School, Glengarra Td.
Reg. 22902120

54 Ballinvella National School, Ballinvella (Cos. By.) Td.
Reg. 22902912

54-55 De La Salle College, Newtown Road, Waterford City Td., Waterford
Reg. 22830013

55 Saint Otteran's Hospital, Grange Road Upper, Waterford City Td., Waterford
Reg. 22830060

56 Dungarvan Union Workhouse, Mitchel Street, Curraheen Commons Td., Dungarvan
Not included in survey

56 Kilmathomas Union Workhouse, Carrignanonshagh Td., Kilmacthomas
Not included in survey

56 Waterford City Union Workhouse, John's Hill/Inner Ring Road, Waterford City Td., Waterford
Not included in survey

56-57 Lismore Union Workhouse, Townparks East (Cos. By.) Lism. Par. Td., Lismore
Reg. 22902116

58 Hannan Flour Mills, Tallow Td., Tallow
Reg. 22818050, 22818063

58-59 Portlaw Cotton Factory, Factory Road (off), Coolroe (Upp. By.) Clonagam Par. Td., Portlaw
Reg. 22803073

58 Mayfield House, Coolroe (Upp. By.) Clonagam Par. Td., Portlaw
Reg. 22803035

60 Clashmore Distillery/Clashmore Flour Mill, Coolbooa Td./Clashmore Td., Clashmore
Reg. 22826003, 22826020

60 Carrigcastle (Corn) Mill, Carrigcastle Td.
Reg. 22902404

60-61 Tankardstown Copper Mine, Knockmahon Td.
Reg. 22902504

61 Osbourne Terrace, Ballynasissala Td., Knockmahon
Reg. 22812026, 13 - 14

61 Copper Mine Manager's House, Knockmahon Td., Knockmahon
Reg. 22812020

61 Saint Mary's Catholic Church, Kilduane Td., Knockmahon
Reg. 22812019

61 Lime kiln, Woodhouse (D. Wt. By.) Strad. Par. Td., Stradbally
Reg. 22811014

62 Cappoquin Market House (Old), Cook Street/Main Street, Cappoquin Td., Cappoquin
Reg. 22810099

62 Moore's Hotel, Main Street, Cappoquin Td., Cappoquin
Reg. 22810064 - 22810065

62-63 Walsh's, Main Street/The Green/Barrack Street, Cappoquin Td., Cappoquin
Reg. 22810041

62-63 Olden, Barrack Street, Cappoquin Td., Cappoquin
Reg. 22810028

62-63 Kenny, Main Street, Cappoquin Td., Cappoquin
Reg. 22810021

62-63 House, Main Street, Cappiquin Td., Cappoquin
Reg. 22810069

64 Twomey and Company, Main Steet, Cappoquin Td., Cappoquin
Reg. 22810066

64 T. Uniacke, Main Street, Cappoquin Td., Cappoquin
Reg. 22810008

64 House, Main Street, Cappoquin Td., Cappoquin
Reg. 22810072

65 House, Main Street/Castle Street, Cappoquin Td., Cappoquin
Reg. 22810017

65-67 Greehy, Main Street, Lismore (Cos. By.) Td., Lismore
Reg. 22809026

65-67 R. Foley/Mall Bar (The), Main Street/North Mall, Lismore (Cos. By.) Td., Lismore
Reg. 22809067

66-67 Arcade (The), 5 - 6 Main Street, Lismore (Cos. By.) Td., Lismore
Reg. 22809005

66-67 Red House Inn (The), Main Street/Chapel Street, Lismore (Cos. By.) Td., Lismore
Reg. 22809032

66 Lismore Courthouse, West Street/Chapel Street, Lismore (Cos. By.) Td., Lismore
Reg. 22809034

66 Lismore Arms Hotel, Main Street/The Square, Lismore (Cos. By.) Td., Lismore
Reg. 22809001

66-67 G. Kee Fabrics, 3 Barrack Street, Waterford City Td., Waterford
Reg. 22502367

65-67 J. and K. Walsh, 11 Great George's Street, Waterford City Td., Waterford
Reg. 22501506

65-67 Frank English, 1 O'Connell Street/Thomas Street, Waterford City Td., Waterford
Reg. 22500264

67 John Hearn, 87 - 88 Coal Quay, Waterford City Td., Waterford
Reg. 22504007

67 An Siopa, 60 John Street/Saint John's Avenue, Waterford City Td., Waterford
Reg. 22501241

67 Siam, 61 John Street, Waterford City Td., Waterford
Reg. 22501240

67 Ginos, 62 John Street, Waterford City Td., Waterford
Reg. 22501239

67 Antiques, 63 John Street, Waterford City Td., Wateford
Reg. 22501238

68 Granary (The)/Waterford City Tourist Office, Merchant's Quay/Hanover Street, Waterford City Td., Waterford
Reg. 22500295

68-69 Assembly House, 31 O'Connell Street, Waterford City Td., Waterford
Reg. 22501065

70-71 FBD Insurance, 1 Great George's Street/Sargent's Lane, Waterford City Td., Waterford
Reg. 22501515

70-71 Waterford Chamber of Commerce/Port of Waterford Company (Morris House), 2 Great George's Street, Waterford City Td., Waterford
Reg. 22501514

70-71 Waterford City Post Office, 100 Custom House Quay/Keizer Street, Waterford City Td., Waterford
Reg. 22504035

71 Clyde House, 107 The Quay/Keizer Street, Waterford City Td., Waterford
Reg. 22504041

72-73 Boyce Cottages, Townparks East (Cos. By.) Tallow Par. Td., Tallow
Reg. 22818051, 22818065 - 22818069

72 Almshouse, Townparks East (Cos. By.) Tallow Par. Td.
Reg. 22902804

72 Waterford County Gaol, Ballybricken Green, Waterford City Td., Waterford
Now gone

72 Waterford Military Barracks, Barrack Street/Green Street/Newport Square, Waterford City Td., Waterford
Reg. 22502156, 22502540, 22502543, 22502989

73 5 O'Connell Street, Waterford City Td., Waterford
Reg. 22500306

73 5 - 21 Green Street, Waterford City Td., Waterford
Reg. 22502135

73 1 - 22 Summerhill Terrace, Waterford City Td., Waterford
Reg. 22500095, 22500104, 22500111, 22500118

73 7 Summerhill Terrace, Waterford City Td., Waterford
Reg. 22500119

74 Catholic Church of the Holy Trinity Without, Ballybricken Green (off)/Mayor's Walk (off), Waterford City Td., Waterford
Reg. 22502069

74 Catholic Church of Saint John the Baptist, Crooke Td., Crooke
Reg. 22901809

75 Killrossanty Church, Gortnalaght Td.
Reg. 22901401

75 Saint Mary's Church, Fountain Td.
Reg. 22902902

75-79 Saint Carthage's Cathedral, North Mall, Lismore (Cos. By.), Lismore
Reg. 22809088

76-77 Gateway, Saint Carthage's Cathedral, North Mall, Lismore (Cos. By.), Lismore
Reg. 22809089

80 Saint John's Church, Ballycahane Td.
Reg. 22900807

80-81 Clonagam Church, Curraghmore Td.
Reg. 22900809

80 Abbey Church, Mount Melleray Monastery, Mountmelleray Td.
Reg. 22902134

80 Seminary, Mount Melleray Monastery, Mountmelleray Td.
Reg. 22902135

80 Farmyard Complex, Melleray Monastery, Mountmelleray Td.
Reg. 22902136

80-81 Boarding Houses, Mount Melleray Monastery, Mountmelleray Td.
Reg. 22902121, 22902128 - 22902132

80-81 Catholic Chapel, Boarding Houses, Mount Melleray Monastery, Mountmelleray Td.
Reg. 22902133

80-83 Presentation Convent, Slievekeale Road, Waterford City Td., Waterford
Reg. 22829002

83 Saint John's Manor, Slievekeale Road, Waterford City Td., Waterford
Reg. 22829018

83 Catholic Church of Saint Helena of the Cross, Glennanore Td.
Reg. 22900601

83 School, Glennanore Td.
Reg. 22900602

83 Catholic Church of the Holy Cross, Priest's Road/Summer Hill, Tramore West Td., Tramore
Reg. 22816038

83 Saint Patrick's Catholic Church, Coolfinn Td., Portlaw
Reg. 22900819

83 Catholic Church of Saints Quan and Broghan, Ballyneal Td., Clonea
Reg. 22802008

84 Saint Saviour's Dominican (Catholic) Church, Bridge Street/O'Connell Street, Waterford City Td., Waterford
Reg. 22500179

84-86 Catholic Cathedral of the Holy Trinity, Barronstrand Street, Waterford City Td., Waterford
Reg. 22501138

86 Saint Catherine's Hall, Catherine Street/Waterside, Waterford City Td., Waterford
Reg. 22504428

86 Waterford Courthouse, Catherine Street, Waterford City Td., Waterford
Reg. 22504492

86-87 Ballynatray House, Ballynatray Demesne Td.
Reg. 22903712

86-89 'Timber Toes' Bridge, Waterford City Td., Waterford
Now gone

88-89 Sion Hill House, Dock Road, Waterford City Td., Waterford
Reg. 22500072

89 Waterford Chamber of Commerce/Port of Waterford Company (Morris House), 2 Great George's Street, Waterford City Td., Waterford
Reg. 22501514

89 Curraghmore House, Curraghmore Td.
Reg. 22900816

89-92 Mayfield House, Coolroe (Upp. By.) Clonagam Par. Td., Portlaw
Reg. 22803035

92 Gate Lodge, Mayfield House, Factory Road, Coolroe (Upp. By.) Clonagam Par. Td., Portlaw
Reg. 22803036

92 Saint Joseph's Convent (Woodlock (House)), Carrick Road, Mayfield or Rocketscastle Td., Portlaw
Reg. 22803001

93 Gate Lodge, Saint Joseph's Convent (Woodlock (House)), Carrick Road, Mayfield or Rocketscastle Td., Portlaw
Now gone

93 Whitfield Court, Dooneen (Mid. By.) Kilmeadan Par. Td.
Reg. 22901711

93 Saint Catherine's Hall, Catherine Street/Waterside, Waterford City Td., Waterford
Reg. 22504428

94-95 Lismore Castle, Lismore (Cos. By.) Td., Lismore
Reg. 22809079

94 Faithlegg House, Faithlegg Td.
Reg. 22901005

95 Salterbridge House, Salterbridge Td.
Reg. 22902114

96 Gateway, Ballysaggartmore House, Barranamanoge Td.
Reg. 22902013

96 Ballysaggartmore House, Barranmanoge Td.
Now gone

96 Gateway, Ballysaggartmore House, Knocknagappul (Cos. By.) Td./Barranamanoge Td.
Reg. 22902014

97 Fortwilliam House, Fortwilliam Td.
Reg. 22902006

98   Clock Tower (The), Meagher's
      Quay/Coal quay, Waterford
      City Td., Waterford
      Reg. 22502675

98-99 Holroyd-Smyth Mausoleum,
       Templemichael Church,
       Templemichael Td.
       Reg. 22903717

98-99 Templemichael Church,
       Templemichael Td.,
       Reg. 22903710

100   Master McGrath Monument,
      Ballymacmague South Td.
      Reg. 22903003

100   Le Poer Tower, Tower Hill,
      Clonagam Td.
      Reg. 22900403

100   Gardenmorris House,
      Gardenmorris Td., Kill
      Reg. 22813009

100- Gateway, Domana House,
101   Mountrivers Td./Affane
      Td./Dromana (D. Wt. By.) Td.
      Reg. 22902919

100   Domana House, Dromana
      (D. Wt. By.) Td.
      Reg. 22902918

102   Saint James's Church, Church
      Lane, Stradbally More Td.,
      Stradbally
      Reg. 22811001

102   Stradbally Rectory, The Square,
      Stradbally More Td.
      Reg. 22811022 - 22811023

102- Gurteen Le Poer,
103   Gurteen Lower Td.
      Reg. 22900208

102   Lismore Castle, Lismore
      (Cos. By.) Td., Lismore
      Reg. 22809079

102- Waterford Castle Hotel
103   (Island Castle), Little Island Td.
      Reg. 22901002

102- Bushfield (House), Gallows Hill/
103   West Street/Ballyanchor Street,
      Lismore (Cos. By.) Td., Lismore
      Reg. 22809126

103   Curraghmore House,
      Curraghmore Td.
      Reg. 22900816

103   Lismore Castle, Lismore
      (Cos. By.) Td., Lismore
      Reg. 22809079

103   Farmyard Complex, Gurteen Le
      Poer, Gurteen Lower Td.
      Reg. 22900206

103   Gurteen Le Poer,
      Gurteen Lower Td.
      Reg. 22900208

104   Annestown House, Annestown
      Td., Annestown
      Reg. 22814013

104   Outbuilding, Annestown
      House, Annestown Td.,
      Annestown
      Reg. 22814013

104   Thatched Cottage, Dunhill Td.,
      Dunhill
      Reg. 22815002

104   Cove Cottage, Nunnery Lane,
      Stradbally More Td., Stradbally
      Reg. 22811009

104- Woodstown House, Woodstown
105   Lower Td.
      Reg. 22901813

104- Thatched Cottage, Gortnadiha
105   Upper Td.
      Reg. 22903602

106- Sallyhene Cottages,
107   Knocknacrohy Td.
      *Reg. 22900818, 22901825 -
      22901831*

107   Strancally Castle, Strancally
      Demesne Td.
      Reg. 22903402

107   Gateway, Strancally Castle,
      Strancally Demesne Td.
      Reg. 22903401

107   Folly, Strancally Castle,
      Strancally Demesne Td.
      Reg. 22903403

107   Estate Worker's Cottage,
      Strancally Castle, Strancally
      Demesne Td.
      Reg. 22903404

107   Farmyard Complex, Strancally
      Castle, Strancally Demesne Td.
      Reg. 22903406

107   Cottage Orné, Strancally Castle,
      Strancally Demesne Td.
      Reg. 22903405

107   Estate Workers' Houses,
      Sapperton House, Sapperton
      South Td.
      Reg. 22902931, 22902932

108   Thatched Cottage,
      Stonehouse Td.
      Reg. 22900805

108   Kilrush Cottage, Kilrush
      (Marquis) Td.
      Reg. 22903101

108   Thatched Cottage,
      Balleighteragh East Td.
      Reg. 22903106

109   Thatched Cottage,
      Ballingown Td.
      Reg. 22902923

109- Thatched Cottage, Garraun Td.
110   *Reg. 22902203*

110   Thatched Cottage,
      Garranturton Td.
      Reg. 22902402

110   Thatched Cottage, Garrarus Td.
      Reg. 22902604

110   Thatched Cottage,
      Ballynakill (D. Wt. By.)
      Reg. 22902305

110- Dromore Cottage, Dromore Td.
111   *Reg. 22903409*

111   Thatched Cottage, Matthew's
      Crossroads, Ballyduff East Td.
      Reg. 22901605

111   Thatched Cottage,
      Ballinattin Td.
      Reg. 22902608

111   Farmhouse, Knockalisheen
      (Glen. By.) Td.
      Reg. 22900605

110- Thatched Farmhouse,
111   Curraheenavoher Td.
      Reg. 22900506

112   Niervale (House), Ballymacarbry
      Td., Ballymacarbry
      Reg. 22801008

112- Outbuildings, Niervale (House),
113   Ballymacarbry Td.,
      Ballymacarbry
      Reg. 22801009 - 22801012

113   Outbuilding, Garrarus Td.
      Reg. 22902604

113   Brook Lodge, Brooklodge Td.
      Reg. 22902202

114   Post Box, Adamstown
      (Mid. By.) Kilmeadan Par. Td.
      The Sweep
      Reg. 22901615

114   Post Box, Glennanore Td.
      Reg. 22900607

114   Post Box, Farnane Upper Td.,
      Millstreet
      Reg. 22902205

114   Plunkett Railway Station
      (Waterford (North) Railway
      Station), Terminus Street,
      Waterford City Td., Waterford
      Reg. 22500032

114   Canopy, Plunkett Railway
      Station (Waterford (North)
      Railway Station), Terminus
      Street, Waterford City Td.,
      Waterford
      Reg. 22500033

114   Signal Box, Plunkett Railway
      Station (Waterford (North)
      Railway Station), Terminus
      Street, Waterford City Td.,
      Waterford
      Reg. 22500027

114   Edmund Rice Bridge, Waterford
      City Td., Waterford
      Reg. 22500075

115   Suir Bridge, Gracedieu East Td.
      Reg. 22900903

115   1 - 7 Western Terrace, Old
      Chapel Lane, Dungarvan Td.,
      Dungarvan
      *Reg. 22821106, 22821107,
      22821167 - 22821171*

115   5 Western Terrace, Old Chapel
      Lane, Dungarvan Td.,
      Dungarvan
      Reg. 22821107

115   6 - 43 O'Connell Street,
Fairlane (D. Wt. By.) Dun. Par.
Td./Gallowshill (D. Wt. By.)
Dun. Par., Dungarvan
Reg. 22821067, 22821068

115   1 - 14 Alexander Street,
Waterford City Td., Waterford
Reg. 22501374

115   11 - 12 Alexander Street,
Waterford City Td., Waterford
Reg. 22501380

116   Ballyduff Carnegie Free Library,
Ballyduff (Cos. By.) Td.,
Ballyduff
Reg. 22808008

116   Lismore Carnegie Free Library,
West Street, Castlelands Td.,
Lismore
Reg. 22809045

116   Tallow Carnegie Free Library,
Convent Street (Tallowbridge
Street), Tallow Td., Tallow
Reg. 22818003

116   Waterford City Carnegie Free
Library, Lady Lane/Bakehouse
Lane, Waterford City Td.
Reg. 22501189

116   Cappoquin Carnegie Free
Library, Main Street,
Cappoquin Td., Cappoquin
Reg. 22810025

116-   Quays (The), 81 Coal Quay,
117   Waterford City Td., Waterford
Reg. 22501115

116-   Clock Tower Dry Cleaners,
117   82 Coal Quay, Waterford City
Td., Waterford
Reg. 22501116

116-   Farrell Travel, 83 Coal Quay,
117   Waterford City Td., Waterford
Reg. 22501117

116-   Grant Hair, 84 Coal Quay,
117   Waterford City Td., Waterford
Reg. 22501118

116-   Bank (The), Gladstone Street/
117   O'Connell Street, Waterford
City Td., Waterford
Reg. 22501066

117   Crane, Custom House Quay,
Waterford City Td., Waterford
Reg. 22504561

117-   R. and H. Hall Flour Mills,
119   Dock Road, Ferrybank Td.,
Waterford
Reg. 22900908

119   Cherry's Brewery, Mary Street,
Waterford City Td., Waterford
Reg. 22500085, 22500385

119   Gardenmorris House,
Gardenmorris Td., Kill
Reg. 22813009

118-   Cappoquin House, Cappoquin
119   Demesne Td., Cappoquin
Reg. 22810098

119   Mount Congreve (House),
Mountcongreve (Mid. By.)
Kilmeadan Par. Td.
Reg. 22901710

119   Watch Tower, Dysert Td.
Reg. 22904010

120   Tony Burke, 9 O'Connell
Street, Waterford City Td.,
Waterford
Reg. 22500303

120   Ormonde Cinema, O'Connell
Street/Stephen's Street, Fairlane
(D. Wt. By.) Dun. Par. Td.,
Dungarvan
Reg. 22821080

120   M.J. Curran, 31 Grattan
Square/O'Connell Street,
Dungarvan Td., Dungarvan
Reg. 22821034

120   Portlaw Cotton Factory, Factory
Road (off), Coolroe (Upp. By.)
Clonagam Par. Td., Portlaw
Reg. 22803073

121   Waterford Baptist Church,
Catherine Street, Waterford
City Td., Waterford
Reg. 22504438

122-   Abbey Church, Mount Melleray
123   Monastery, Mountmelleray Td.
Reg. 22902134

123   Catholic Church of the Sacred
Heart, Richardson's Folly/Lower
Grange Road, Waterford City
Td., Waterford
Reg. 22830211

124   Waterford Town Hall and
Theatre Royal, The Mall,
Waterford City Td., Waterford
Reg. 22504135

124   Granary (The)/Waterford City
Tourist Office, Merchant's
Quay/Hanover Street, Waterford
City Td., Waterford
Reg. 22500295

124   Dungarvan Museum, Friary
Street (Saint Augustine Street),
Dungarvan Td., Dungarvan
Reg. 22821122

124   Houses, George's Street,
Coolroe (Upp. By.) Clonagam
Par. Td., Portlaw,
Not included in survey

124   Killoteran Church,
Killoteran Td.
Reg. 22901706

124   Gate Lodge. Salterbridge House,
Fadduaga Td.
Reg. 22902112

124   Salterbridge House,
Salterbridge Td.
Reg. 22902114

Acknowledgements

NIAH
Senior Architect Willy Cumming
Survey Controller Damian Murphy
Survey Manager Marc Ritchie
GIS Technician TJ O'Meara
Additional NIAH Staff Flora O'Mahony, Gareth John, Mildred Dunne, Erika Sjöberg and Barry O'Reilly

The NIAH gratefully acknowledges the following in the preparation of the Waterford County Survey and Introduction:

Survey Fieldwork
Alastair Coey Architects in association with Howley Harrington Architects.

Recorders
Alastair Coey, James Howley, Ross Hart, Gareth Hutchinson, Sharon Brown, Brian Turner, Jill Kerry, Alan Dorman, Anne Coey, Ruth Thompson, Janet Lunn, Alyson Carney, Adrian Curran, Emmeline Henderson, Fred Hammond, Helen Hossack, Olwyn James, Chris McCollum, Tom McGimpsey, Audrey McGrath, Christopher Moriarty, Eimear O'Connell, Jane O'Halloran, James Shine and David Smith.

Introduction
Writers Jane Fenlon and Hugh Maguire
Editor Hugh Maguire
Copy Editor Eleanor Flegg
Translator Context
Photographer Patrick Donald
Designed by Bennis Design
Printed by Colourprint

The NIAH wishes to thank all of those who allowed access to their property for the purpose of the Waterford County Survey and subsequent photography. The NIAH wishes to acknowledge Sr. Perpetua Gannon, Presentation Convent, Waterford, Mr. Seán O'Brien, Woodview House, Portlaw, Ms. R. Yalaahst, Dunhill, Ms. Uí Teanchú, Portlaw, Ms. Anne Brennock, Lismore Castle, Mr. Michael Penruddock, Lismore Castle, Anna Meenan, Cecily Johnson, David Davison and Garry Miley.

The NIAH also wishes to acknowledge the generous assistance given by the staff of The Heritage Council, the Irish Architectural Archive (IAA), the Mills and Millers Society of Ireland, the National Library of Ireland (NLI), the National Gallery of Ireland (NGI), the Waterford City Archive, the Waterford Museum of Treasures, the Cork Public Museum, and Trinity College Dublin.

Sources of Illustrations
All of the original photographs for the Introduction were taken by Patrick Donald. The illustrations listed below are identified by their figure number:

12, 22,28, 32, 70, 71, 109, 126, 136, and archival images on pages 2, 14, and 94 courtesy of the Irish Architectural Archive (IAA); archival image on page. 2 from Ryland, Rev. R.H., The History, Topography and Antiquities of the County and City of Waterford (London, 1824); 19, 36, 28, 45, 72, 73, 74, 125, 133, 183, and archival images on pages 5, 20, 35, 43, 44, 45, 46, 47, 63, 72, 83, and 93 are the property of the National Library of Ireland and have been reproduced with the permission of the Council of Trustees of the National Library of Ireland (NLI); 14 and archival image on page 15 courtesy of the National Gallery of Ireland (NGI); archival images on page 7 reproduced courtesy of the Waterford Museum of Treasures; archival image on page 24 courtesy of the Waterford City Archives; archival image on page 46 reproduced from a map in Trinity College Library Dublin, by permission of the Board of Trinity College; 111 courtesy of Cork Public Museum; 1, and 2 reproduced courtesy of the photographic unit of the Department of the Environment, Heritage and Local Government; 93, and 94 courtesy of Myrtle Allen, Allen Collection, County Cork.

The NIAH has made every effort to source and acknowledge the owners of all of the archival illustrations included in this Introduction. The NIAH apologises for any omissions made, and would be happy to include such acknowledgements in future issues of this Introduction.

Please note that the majority of the structures included in the Waterford County Survey are privately owned and are therefore not open to the public.

ISBN: 0755719115
© *Government of Ireland 2004*

Questionnaire

Name:

Address:

Email:

Age: 10 - 18   18 -30   30 - 50   50 - 65   65+

Occupation:

Did you purchase this publication for: General interest   Professional use

Comments / Suggestions / Corrections:

The information in this questionnaire is to provide a feedback to the NIAH.
It will be kept confidential and will not given to any other authority.

The NIAH survey of the architectural heritage of County Waterford can be accessed on the internet at: **www.buildingsofireland.ie** The data accessible on the internet includes a written record and images of each of the sites included in the NIAH survey. However, the mapping data, indicating the location of each site surveyed, is not available on the NIAH website.

If you would like to receive the mapping on CD-ROM please complete this questionnaire and send it with a stamped addressed envelope, large enough to hold a CD, to NIAH, Dún Scéine, Harcourt Lane, Dublin 2.